HOW I TOPPED THE
BOARDS
AND YOU CAN TOO!

Gaurav Sood graduated from The Doon School as the all-India ISC Board examination topper in 2008. He secured 99 per cent, the highest marks in India's history, and was felicitated with various national awards.

He then did his bachelor's in Economics at St Stephen's College, where he secured the most-sought-after campus-recruitment offer—a role as one of the youngest management consultants at McKinsey & Company.

Gaurav then took his GMAT and TOEFL exams, where he got a near-perfect 780 and a perfect 120, respectively, and is currently on a full scholarship at the University of Oxford.

In his free time, Gaurav can either be found trying to (unsuccessfully) emulate Roger Federer on the tennis court or tormenting people in the vicinity with his music, under the name Rooftop Sundays. He's also a terrible cook, who, by some miracle, once managed to explode five eggs. Understandably, he's now banned from his mother's kitchen.

HOW I TPPED THE
BOARDS
AND YOU CAN TOO!

Gaurav Sood

RUPA

Published by
Rupa Publications India Pvt. Ltd 2019
7/16, Ansari Road, Daryaganj
New Delhi 110002

Sales centres:
Allahabad Bengaluru Chennai
Hyderabad Jaipur Kathmandu
Kolkata Mumbai

ISBN: 978-93-5333-333-1

First impression 2019

10 9 8 7 6 5 4 3 2 1

The moral right of the author has been asserted.

Printed by Parksons Graphics Pvt. Ltd., Mumbai

Dedicated to my mum and dad...
and to my younger brother, who got the remaining 1%.

Contents

The Chapter That No One Reads: The Preface

As an Indian student, the boards will possibly be the most important examination of your life. The exams you take over that one month will determine the direction your life will take—the college gates you walk through, the job you get, the relations you form... Not many exams have that ability.

I'm often asked what I did to top the boards.

'You must be really smart!'

'Did you have to study twenty-four hours a day?'

'Are you some kind of freaky genius?'

Those are just a bunch of the questions that have come my way since I topped the boards in 2008.

I'll be the first to admit that I've never really been an exceptionally gifted student. I'll admit I was a decent student all my life, but anything north of *decent* would be pushing it, as far as adjectives to describe my intellect are concerned.

Sure, I worked hard, but I neither was, nor am the most hard-working person you'll ever meet. Did I work a lot for the board exams? Most certainly—I put in a lot more effort for the board exams than I did for any other exam in my life. But were there people around me who put in more effort than I did? Even more certainly.

And no, I'm most certainly not a freaky genius. Of any kind.

So how, then, did I, a normal kid, manage to top the boards across India? More importantly, how can you?

Could it be that I got plain lucky? Perhaps. But how, then, did I find myself studying in The Doon School—one of the most difficult in India to secure admission in—to begin with? How did I manage a near-perfect 780 GMAT and a perfect 120 TOEFL score? How did I find myself at the doorstep of McKinsey & Company, the management-consulting giant that moulds more CEOs than any other company? How did I get a full scholarship to the University of Oxford?

You see, it's all about connecting the dots—the little things, so to say. You don't need to be a prodigy to ace an exam—you just need to work smart. This book will do just that—it will help you connect the dots by listing out the methods, tips and tricks that allowed me to top the boards, so that you can best prepare for the most important exam of your life.

In this book, I've detailed how I went about preparing for the national ISC exam—what I studied, how I studied, how I paced myself, etc.—the methods that helped me top the boards and can hopefully help you do the same. There are things in here that seem obvious in retrospect, but it's surprising how often kids struggle to 'figure it out' in the moment.

This book has been written for students and parents alike, so that students who read it can give the national board examinations their best shot and consequently maximize their results, while parents who read it can understand what to expect during this period and how best to drive this process and make the journey as smooth as possible for their child.

PS: If I'm being honest, the best question that's ever been hurled at me as far as the boards are concerned was from my best friend, who heard the news and just mumbled one garbled word while continuing to munch on his greasy slice of pizza:

'You?!!'

If you ever come across me, you'll probably scratch your head as well, while a puzzled, almost contorted, expression involuntarily forms on your face and a single word pops up in your mind:

'Him?!!'

1

My Story

Right off the bat, I should get something out of the way—I'm not the smartest person you'll ever bump into. This isn't a story about a child genius. I was a normal kid growing up. Average, really. I wasn't the top of my class. I tanked a lot of exams. I've been at the receiving end of a fair share of lectures from my parents for grades that could embarrass our entire neighbourhood. I was that kid who was bright—you know, the kid who was supposed to do well—the top 10 per cent of the class, but nothing exceptional, really. That was me, pretty much.

Even before I was born, my parents, with exceptional foresight, correctly anticipated what an absolute delight I'd be to raise during my years of adolescence, and knew that it would be a crime to deprive other lucky souls of my tantrums. So the plan was to pack me up and ship me off to boarding school smack in the middle of my most charming years—puberty. Philanthropy has many forms.

If I were to be a girl, mum wanted me to go to Welham Girls' School—the one she had studied in. If I were to be a boy, I was to go to The Doon School—the one my dad had *not* studied in. Unfortunately, dad wasn't granted a vote. Mum was quite adamant in her choices and defended them vociferously. She now claims she was completely rational, even polite, at the time, but bystanders secretly disagree with her narration of events. One brave soul, though, came forward many years later and said that 'even the orcs of *The Lord of the Rings* would have been easier to reason with'. That, incidentally, was my father. He regrets his act of bravery to this day.

Anyway, I turned out to be (and still am) a boy, and was registered at birth for The Doon School entrance examination, to be held twelve years later.

Somehow, I exceeded expectations and managed to survive that examination. I was a Dosco, whatever that meant. I was just excited that I would finally get to play cricket with a red leather ball, with the big boys on a big pitch (I'd write a book about my cricketing career, but that would end in a single line—clean bowled). My parents were thrilled and laddus were distributed to everyone—even to the neighbours who lived three doors down.

So, like I said, I was never the brightest kid in class. I gave my 12th-grade ISC Board examinations and trotted off to Mumbai to spend the summer composing and recording music with my best friend. I was happy with the way the exams had gone. For a change, I had worked hard and expected a great result.

I most certainly did not expect to hear my friend shouting that I was on the news. I was playing on his fancy new PlayStation when I heard him yell my name. With all my attention focused squarely on trying to ensure that my name didn't pop up in the *Guinness Book of World Records* for losing the game in record time, I wasn't really paying attention to what he was yelling. All I understood was that the board results were out.

The one cardinal rule of gaming is that no self-respecting gamer pauses a game midway. So I yelled back at him, telling him to relax for a few minutes while I— and I quote—*destroyed my opponent.* I didn't have to wait long—I lost the game ten seconds later. Magnanimous in defeat, muttering to myself that my opponent only won because he got lucky, I tossed the remote aside, got up from the sofa and turned on the computer to check my results.

According to my calculation, I should have scored a 97 per cent. I was pretty darn satisfied. I wasn't sure why my friend was still yelling, though. So I walked into the room to find my acned face splashed across NDTV, with the scroll reading: *'Gaurav Sood of The Doon School, Dehradun, tops the ISC 12th-Grade Board Examinations with a 99 per cent.'*

Hold on a second. 99 per cent?

They'd clearly got something wrong there. There was no way I was *that* smart.

Turns out I wasn't, because the 'All-India Topper' had just made a mistake calculating his own best-of-five percentage, which should have been a 99 per cent, as opposed to the 97 per cent he had arrived at, somehow. That should have been the first red flag—that the topper didn't deserve that 100 in Math...

∿

After my brief tryst with celebrity life, having been unceremoniously thrust in front of news cameras, interviewers and journalists, it was time for normal life to resume. Still full to the brim with every possible form of celebratory sweets, mum decided that *rajma chawal* on my eighteenth birthday was in everyone's best dietary interests. And with that meal came the time to decide where to go to college. My marks had opened up a whole host of opportunities. For example, I was granted the course of my choice at BITS Pilani, without even having to give the entrance exam, which I thought was pretty *awesome*.

Maybe I was just tired of having spent the last six years of my life in a boarding school surrounded by a bunch of smelly guys, but I wasn't exactly looking forward to four more years of the same at engineering college.

Mum was an Economics lecturer back in the day, so it made sense that I hated economics for a good part of my student life. It was only in Class 11, or *S-Form*, as we Doscos call it, that it all came together during a discussion about Samuelson and the law of diminishing returns that, against insurmountable odds, I managed to stay awake through.

Looking back, that was the day everything clicked. I stopped sleeping through Economics class and my face stopped resembling a blank canvas. All of a sudden, everything that I had previously dismissed as gibberish started to make sense, and I began loving the subject. There was no looking back from there. My heart had decided: economics. And I had decided where I wanted to study—St Stephen's College, Delhi, India's most reputed for the course.

Plus, I figured that all those years I'd spent learning the guitar could finally be put to more productive use serenading girls instead.

St Stephen's is one of the few colleges that have their own interview process. So I began preparing for it. Having analysed its admissions criteria with a fervour I didn't know I possessed, I was fairly confident I would make the cut. I was slightly less confident when my interviewer (the legendary Professor Raghunathan, in case there are any Stephanians reading this) told me that he'd see me in Pilani.

Somehow, I got the seat. All of a sudden I was a Stephanian—an Economics student at St Stephen's College. At Stephen's I met some of the most amazing people—people who were genuinely smart, who inspired me, who pushed me to become better. People who didn't just do something because it looked good on a résumé, but because it was the right thing to do.

I found myself introduced to the opposite sex for the first time, which, for a kid from an all-boys boarding school, was a pretty big deal. My first meaningful interaction with a particularly pretty girl was, I'm told, a garble of stammers and incoherent syllables that I was attempting to pass off as the English language. It couldn't have been all that bad, though, because that incredible girl became the rock in my life for the next eight years.

Over those three years, I made some of my best friends (to this day) and was truly happy. I had worked hard to be where I wanted to be, I was surrounded by the most amazing people in the world and was lucky to be in a wonderful relationship with a beautiful girl who also happened to be my best friend. It helped that I was also doing well in college. I was busy with society work—I had joined several clubs and was heavily involved in music. A bunch of us had formed a college band that we called U.8. Noise—a fairly appropriate moniker, given that we aurally traumatized most of U Block, Mukherji West in the name of practice sessions. We weren't terrible, but we weren't all that great either. We found out a few months in that our drummer was half-deaf, which explained a fair amount about why we were so often out of tempo. But by then, it was too late and we were comfortable with our brand of musical mediocrity. The rest of the time, I could be found in the gym or on the tennis court, unsuccessfully emulating tennis legend Roger Federer's backhand, headband and all.

Come third year, and it was recruitment time. With a near-perfect 780 GMAT and a perfect 120 TOEFL score, I found myself at the doorstep of McKinsey & Company, the management-consulting giant. Now, McKinsey & Company is notoriously picky about selecting its consultants. In India, it recruits just a handful of students from the three IITs, the National Law School of India University (NLSIU), Lady Shri Ram College (LSR) and St Stephen's College—the elitist of the elite, as they like to call it behind closed doors. It was a name that could open any door in the corporate world. It was a label that raised eyebrows. And I was one of the youngest consultants there at the time. I didn't really understand it back then, but the profile that I had got without an

MBA degree was a much bigger deal than I realized. All I knew at the time was that I was being paid more money than I knew what to do with. And I was quickly running out of overpriced guitars to buy...

So, for the purposes of this book, that's pretty much me on a piece of paper. And you might think that it all started with the ISC results and kept rolling from there. And you'd be right to a certain extent. But the truth is that it all started a while before that. I'm going to tell you my story. And sure, there will be many things written here that may seem obvious or generic, but they worked for me—a totally normal kid—and I'm willing to bet that you'll find a few things here that will work for you as well.

So on with the parade, shall we...?

P.S.

2

The Fun Stuff

So before we get to the boring bits, let's talk about the fun stuff.

Go fail a few classes... All of Class 11, if need be.

Alright, don't fail...but you get the drift, which is basically this—*go have some fun. Go do something stupid while you have the time, and get it out of the system.*

I can't stress this enough. Your boards are possibly the most important examination of your life. That one month, for most of you, will determine your path over the next few years, if nothing more. They're important. The sooner you understand that, the better.

We can whine and whine about it as much as we like, but the Indian education system is structured in a way that some exams are more important than the others. In fact, if we look at it, most of life is. It sounds great on paper to say that we should study for the sake of knowledge and not just for an exam. And on most occasions, I would be the first to agree with you— something that isn't done for the right reasons isn't worth doing at the end of the day. Study not for an exam, but for the knowledge. Study not because you have to, but because you want to. Don't study for the marks, study for the learning.

But as poetic as all of that sounds, the fact of the matter is that, for most of us, that strategy doesn't work. That perspective is great for our long-term personal development, but for our purposes, we need to set it aside for a while. Just a while.

You see, there are very few who will be able to sustain that optimum level over the course of their lives, where they have enough in the tank to crack every examination

'Don't worry, it's just a year of board exams. Then three years of college, a few years of work experience, two more for an MBA, then a stable job, then marriage and kids. After that you're free to follow your passions.'

they take or jump every hurdle that comes their way. Most of us will have our ebbs and flows, and our highs and lows.

Picture yourself at the start of a race, knees bent, waiting for the sound of that pistol. It's a marathon, not a sprint. What's your strategy? Do you go racing out of the blocks at full speed and try to sustain that for the next few hours? Or do you hold back for some time and then give it everything you've got in the final hurdle?

Option 1 sounds great, if you can manage it. In fact, let's imagine that we have Usain Bolt, the legendary sprinter who's trying his luck at the marathon this year. He's sprinted at 100 per cent all his life, and that's his strategy for the marathon as well. And his thought process would be justified—there's no person on this planet who can sprint faster than him.

But this isn't a 100-metre dash. And his opponent in the marathon today is Mo Farah, the most successful British long-distance runner in Olympic history.

Farah understands the limits of his body. He knows there's no way he's faster than Bolt. He's never beating him in a sprint. But what he has over Bolt is stamina. He's happy to let him take the lead at the start—because the only thing that matters is the finish.

So who do you think will win this race? The person who's planning to sprint his way through the marathon or the person who has the right strategy for a marathon?

Now if Bolt can, in fact, sprint at 100 per cent through the course of the entire marathon, there's nothing that Farah can do, except say *'too good'* and concede defeat to someone who is as close to Superman as we'll ever get. There would be no shame in that defeat.

But the odds are that Bolt, for all his incredible talent, isn't Superman. And life is all about the odds. The odds are that Bolt will run out of steam—and Farah knows it. And so he's happy to let Bolt take the lead and tire himself out at the beginning. And slowly but surely, Farah will catch up and, eventually, win that race. And like I said, it's only the finishing line that matters.

It's exactly the same in life—and for our purposes, the board examinations. If you're going to try to ace every exam, big or small that comes before you, eventually you're going to burn out. I've seen it happen to some of the most talented and brilliant individuals that I know. I wasn't a patch on them academically, but whenever it mattered, I outran them comprehensively, and then some.

To give you another analogy, I'm going to swing into the world of tennis—my favourite sport and way to pass time and destroy television remotes (tennis can be an expensive vocation when you've woken up at 3 a.m. on a work day to watch a four-hour match, only for your favourite player to lose at the end of it). You might have heard of Roger Federer, the legendary Swiss tennis player? Do you know why Federer is considered the greatest tennis player, and perhaps athlete, of all time? Not because of the number of total titles or matches he's won. He's second on that list. Most average enthusiasts won't even recognize the name of the person who holds that record. But in tennis, the biggest titles are the Grand Slams—four held every year. Those are the titles that count—that define a tennis player's legacy and his or her place in the record books. Federer has won more of these titles than any other male player in the game. That's what makes him such a legend. In tennis circles, it's widely agreed that there is no one better than him at pacing himself or herself to be in optimum shape for the Grand Slams. He uses the rest of the tournaments to sharpen his tools for these four that matter.

It's nearly impossible for us to bring our A-game every single day. It's unrealistic to expect that of ourselves. The solution? We need to pace ourselves to perform our best when it matters the most. In our case, it's the board examinations.

If you've exhausted most of your reserves preparing for your 11th-grade school examinations, chances are that, by the time your far-more-important final year comes around, you won't be in shape to give it your 100 per cent. Burnt out may be too strong a word, but you get the drift. Anything short of your 100 per cent is not going to get you the results you want.

Mentally, you want to be as fresh as possible coming into your 12th grade. So our preparation begins a year before—that's the bad news. The good news? The preparation is to have as much fun as possible. Yup. Go join the clubs you want to. Learn the guitar. Watch as many reruns of *Game of Thrones* as you like the night before a test. Waste as much time as you can with your friends. That's basically it. We're playing the long game, and we're playing to win. And if we want to win, we need to charge our batteries and get everything out of our system before the 12th grade comes around.

Like Mo Farah, and Roger Federer, even while taking it easy, we're subconsciously getting ready for the final stretch. It'll be here sooner than you know, and when it does, you'll be ready.

High school in a nutshell

PICK ANY 3:

☐ GOOD GRADES
☐ EXTRA CURRICULARS
☐ SOCIAL LIFE
☐ ENOUGH SLEEP

3

Perspective

It was 2007, and I had just joined Class 12. It was the summer vacation and much to my mum's dismay, I was back home from boarding school for the next two months. At the time, there was still approximately a year to go for the board examinations.

I always loved summer vacation, because it meant that my birthday was around the corner. And birthdays meant cake and presents. My birthday also meant that it was the one day of the year I could do pretty much what I wanted and get away with it.

That year, on my birthday, I had a few friends sleeping over. They turned up in the evening, sloppily dressed as ever, and we decided to order food and watch a movie. Now, maybe it was because the movie of choice was *The Exorcist*, but in about ten minutes flat, I was nowhere to be found. And because I had the best friends in the world, they didn't even realize that the birthday boy had gone missing until that absolutely terrifying demon had been successfully exorcized two mortifying hours later. When they did amble out of the TV room, they found me holed up in my study, taking notes. On my birthday. For an exam that was one year away.

I distinctly remember words like '*nerd*' being thrown around.

Did it bother me? Nope. Not for a second. I smiled and shrugged it off. Why didn't I allow it to trouble me? I was a seventeen-year-old with anger-management issues that could give footballer Zinedine Zidane a run for his money. If the past were any precedent, I would fly off the handle and sulk for hours. It's not like I was taking Zen 101 lessons in my spare time.

Early in the year, I had told myself that come Class 12, I was going to give the next year everything I had. I'd had my fun over the previous year, and I was bristling to go. In fact, because I hadn't studied seriously in twelve months, I was actually looking forward to getting back to my books, so much so that the prospect of sitting through 500 pages of Organic Chemistry didn't seem as mind-numbingly terrible as it did enjoyable. That's how effective my time off the previous year had been.

I knew just how important the board examinations were if I wanted to have any shot at getting into a great college. And as much as it sucked, I knew that this one exam would determine my next few years, if nothing else. I'm always the first to admit that a single exam—or a number—for that matter, can in no way be a barometer of a person's calibre—we're too complex to be defined by a single number. Almost every day I bump into someone who's far smarter than I can ever hope to be, and in a moment that adroitly combines envy and self-pity, I think to myself, '*Damn, I wish I could add 73 and 89 as fast as he can. That way I'd never get ripped off by the sabzi bhaiyya again.*' I have no delusions of self-grandeur. Not once have I believed that my 99 per cent makes me smarter than the rest of the world. Or well, technically, India. And neither should you.

But I did understand the importance of those marks. The marks you get in your board exams will allow you to choose your college. The better your marks, the more choices you will have, and any economist will tell you that the more choice you have, the better it is. Your college will allow you to choose your job. You'll meet your best friends along the way. You'll probably have your heart broken a few times on that journey. And maybe you'll eventually meet that girl. So, no, your marks will never define you. No single number or exam ever will. But they'll open doors to experiences that will. It's a subtle distinction, but an important one nevertheless.

During my time as a management consultant at McKinsey, I asked someone far smarter than me why marks were such an important parameter for companies. He said that the marks were a signal; so were the college and the achievements. Recruiters are aware that there may be the perfect candidate out there somewhere— someone who maybe never got the marks and hence the chance to go to that fancy college. But companies don't have the time or the resources to go on the quest for that '*perfect*' candidate. And frankly, they don't need to. Your marks, your college, your extracurriculars—they are all signals that tell a recruiter that you're probably good enough to earn them a lot of money (trust me, it's a lot more than they pay us).

Think of it like a sieve—the exam filters out the 'good' cookies and separates them from the 'bad', as crass as that sounds. Of course, there is a margin for error. Some good cookies will get stuck in the sieve, while some bad ones will flow through. But then there'll be another sieve, maybe in the form of a college exam, and then another and another, and eventually you'll end up with a fairly yum cookie pile.

So sure, go ahead and be sceptical about exams. But don't lose sight of the perspective. All said and done, they are important, so don't screw them up! It's a continuous cycle, but we'll get to that in another chapter.

> *The elevator to success is out of order.*
> *You'll have to use the stairs, one step at a time.*
>
> —JOE GIRARD

4

There's No Way Around the Hard Work. So Embrace It, and Then Some

The day I left for boarding school, my dad sat me down and told me something that has stayed with me ever since. He said, '*Son, whatever you do in life, do it with passion.*' Words that I've tried to live by, albeit with varying degrees of success.

Like I mentioned before, my friends found me holed up in my room on my birthday, studying for an exam that was nearly a year away. Academically, I was an above-average-ish kid. But I knew my strengths, I knew my limitations, I knew my goals and I knew exactly what

I had to do to achieve them. I was willing to put in the effort, and when it came down to it, I did. At the end of the day, there isn't really any magic formula to it—there's nothing anyone or I can tell you that you won't already know. And the truth is that you probably already know the answer. Fortunately or unfortunately, it's pretty simple—nothing beats good ol' hard work at the end of the day.

Yup, mum and dad are always right, as much as you may hate to admit it.

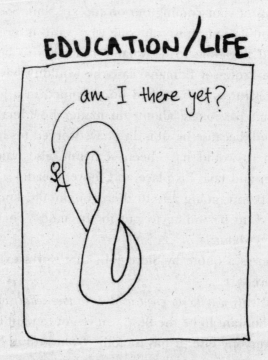

You see, everyone works his or her heart out today, so there really isn't any substitute for perseverance. A few years back, I was talking to Alex Edmans, a famous professor at the London Business School, about his decision to switch from the high-paying world of corporate finance to the slightly less monetarily rewarding world of academia. He began telling me about the importance of being passionate about whatever you do, and he said something that really resonated with me. The gist of his conversation was that if you aren't working your hardest, the odds of your coming out on top are slim. Sooner or later, you'll bump into someone who wants it more than you and is willing to do whatever it takes to beat you to it. In Professor Edmans' case, he wouldn't have been as successful as he was, had he remained in a job that he wasn't passionate about, no matter how lucrative it appeared, because he wouldn't have worked his hardest. And there would have been someone else waiting to jump in and take his place and move ahead.

So before going any further, you should know that you have to be willing to put in the miles. There's no two ways about it.

There's a quote by Steve Jobs that works extremely well here:

'The only way to do great work is to love what you do.'

If you want to be the best, you've got to want it more than everyone else. It has to come from within. No one can force it. Until you want it, it's not going to happen.

Having said that, how often have we seen people work their hearts out only to stay slap-bang at the centre of mediocrity? Because almost everyone gives it their best shot, just giving your best often isn't enough. You need to have a plan. You need to have a goal. You need to know what you need to do to achieve that goal. Most importantly, you have to work smart and connect the dots.

Since I'm a tennis addict, I'm going to give another tennis analogy. What makes Roger Federer the greatest tennis player, if not athlete on the planet? (The analogy can work just as well for Sachin Tendulkar in cricket.) The professional tennis circuit has some incredible athletes. There can be some deep in the Top 100 who can serve faster than Federer; have bigger forehands than Federer; or be fitter and faster than him. Federer has never had the most lethal serve, nor the most devastating backhand. There will be a hundred players on the circuit, most of whom you will never even have heard of, who can hit a forehand harder than him. They can be the most fearful dispatcher of the tennis ball, and yet spend a good part of their career in anonymity.

So what is it that makes Federer so much better than these incredible athletes?

Before the days I really got invested in the world of tennis, I remember a conversation I had with a friend who was then in our school tennis team. Scoffing, I made him aware of my ample scepticism of the sport. I, in a moment of sagely wisdom (common during that, thankfully short, period of my life), stated that tennis was all about luck. One millimetre to the left and the ball would be called out, and one millimetre to the opposite side and you could be hoisting the Wimbledon trophy over your head. There was no way anything but luck, as opposed to the tennis player's skill, could determine that outcome. That's when his offhand reply changed my perspective, not only on tennis but on life as a whole.

'It isn't about luck. That's just how good you have to be.'

Over time, as I got better at tennis and began following the habits of professional players with a more discerning eye, I began to see what he meant. Tennis is a sport where a millimetre separates the legends from the runners-up that nobody remembers. That's how fine the margins are in professional tennis, as they are in everything else in life that's done at a high level. Tennis, for example, is as much mental as it is physical. It isn't all about brute power and strength. You have to be able to handle the stress and the nerves at crucial points. Federer may not have the biggest weapons in the game, not by a long shot, but he does have them all—something you can say for only a handful of players. Above all, what he does better than everybody else is connect the dots through his understanding of the game. He doesn't just work hard, he works smart. He plays to his strengths—that's what makes him the greatest athlete of all time.

There's much we can apply to our lives watching him play. And I can say this with authority, because whenever I've connected the dots, the results have been for everyone to see. Those are the dots I'm trying to share with you.

The journey isn't going to be easy. There are going to be ups and downs. There will be days when you question the use of the effort you're putting in. There will be days when you won't get the results you want. But stick with it.

Since this is a chapter of quotations and tennis analogies, allow me the liberty of one more. There was a Swiss tennis player who had the most gorgeous single-handed backhand. He was talented, and he worked hard. And everyone knew how good he was. But no one recognized him, because his name wasn't Roger Federer. He would always come up second to Federer on the biggest stage. But he never gave up. He believed, and he kept working hard to improve. He had moments when he questioned whether it was even worth it, but he overcame those moments of self-doubt and kept giving every game his best. All while never being resentful of the fame his far-more-successful Swiss countryman enjoyed.

And one day he did come out of the shadow of

being second-best. He now has an Olympic Gold Medal, three Grand Slam titles (and counting), and will go down in the tennis hall of fame when he retires. That's Stanislas *Stan-the-man* Wawrinka for you. And tattooed on his arm is a beautiful quotation by Samuel Beckett that has now become my favourite for various different reasons:

> 'Ever tried, ever failed, no matter.
> Try again, fail again, fail better.'

5

Okay, So Now What?

Just saying something like 'work hard' can be pretty vague and frustratingly unhelpful. And since I don't want you to gouge my eyes out for leaving you with similarly unhelpful advice that isn't actionable, allow me to narrow down what I mean when I use the words *hard work*.

I used to hate taking notes. I hated it ever since the day I grudgingly picked up a pen and saw the monstrosity of a scribble that was supposed to be my 'handwriting'. It was terrifying in its illegibility—almost as frightening as the ten minutes of *The Exorcist* I was brave enough to endure from the safe confines of my blanket on my birthday.

It didn't help that I was born with a condition called hyperhidrosis—a fancy word for sweaty palms. I hated shaking hands with people because it was embarrassing. I didn't want them to know that I had leaky faucets instead of hands. I was constantly drying my palms on my trousers. Most people who saw me probably thought that I really liked caressing my own bums.

But if shaking hands was bad, writing was worse. Within minutes; my notebook could go on eBay for a swimming pool. I tried placing handkerchiefs between my hand and the paper, and I even tried those plastic gloves doctors wear—but nothing helped. Eventually, I just had to grin and bear it, and my teachers had to accept puddles instead of papers. Boy, did I look forward to exams in the Indian summer!

So, yeah, it's safe to say that I hated writing more than most.

But if there was one thing that helped me score the marks I did, I'd be hard-pressed to find a bigger reason than taking notes and compiling them into a single source of reference. I'm not kidding—I stopped referring to my textbooks about six months before my board examinations.

I realized the benefits of taking notes fairly late. It didn't help that writing was a chore for me. Plus, for the longest time, I thought that I was 'too cool to be seen taking notes'. Taking notes was for plebs—the smart kids didn't need to write something down to remember! I would have rather got my arms waxed one excruciating square inch at a time than take notes. And I have fairly hirsute arms.

In Class 11, I had a teacher who seemed to have made it his life's mission to make me take notes. And try as I might, even at my persuasive best, I wasn't able to convince him otherwise. So, resigned to my fate, I took down those notes, one agonizing letter at a time, at every moment thinking to myself, '*What a waste of time.*'

And then the time came for a class test. And instead of having to stay up all night tearing my hair out, I found myself surprisingly at ease with the test syllabus. Even more so, while writing my exam, I didn't find myself struggling to decide what to write. For possibly the first time, my hand knew exactly what to make the pen do, without any hesitancy, hemming or hawing. I was on autopilot, and I barely even realized it. I flew through the test, acing it, and then some.

That was the day I first realized the power of taking notes.

Taking notes helped me in a number of ways.

1. First, it was a great way to reinforce whatever I had studied.
2. It forced me to read the source material slowly, as opposed to skimming through it.

Slower = Better, on most occasions.

3. It allowed me to refer to different textbooks, choose the best parts and compile everything that was relevant into a single note.

4. By the end, I had to refer to just a single notebook, as opposed to a 500-page textbook.

5. It got me comfortable with writing, which really helped during the exams, where I didn't have to waste any time thinking about how I wanted to frame my answer. Plus, by the time the exams came around, I knew exactly how much time it would take me to tackle each question. I never ended up spending more time than required on any answer.

6. My writing = familiar. This helped make the studying process feel more personal, and tailored just for me and my requirements.

Those are some of the reasons I would highly advocate taking notes. Assuming that you're convinced, the next few chapters will explain how we're going to go about this.

> *I find that the harder I work,
> the more luck I seem to have.*
>
> —THOMAS JEFFERSON

6

Step 1: Strategize and Plan

Do you know what the first day of my preparation looked like (this is assuming that it's the beginning of the year and there's plenty of time to go)?

I just looked at the chapter lists of each subject. That's it.

I looked at the chapter list, tried to envision what the exam would potentially look like and put the book away. I then sat back, closed my eyes (okay, I admit that's probably a little dramatic, but I have done that on occasion) and just thought.

The one thing that every person I've spoken to who's topped an exam does is develop his or her strategy and timelines for the rest of the year. That's one thing that every topper has in common.

Planning and strategy—two simple words that can spell the crucial difference between doing your best and doing pretty well—the secret recipe of every person who has ever topped an exam, if you will.

The thing is that we all have our strengths and weaknesses. There are certain subjects that come naturally to us, and certain subjects that require effort. It, therefore, requires a little bit of bespoke tailoring on our part to customize our preparation to complement our skills and bridge our gaps. There's no *one size fits all* approach.

Broadly, there are four options that I would recommend for this step:

1. I find it best to start with a subject that I find the easiest, get my confidence up and then tackle the subject that I find the most difficult. It's something that works for me.
2. Maybe you prefer starting with the hardest subjects and getting those out of the way while you're still fresh.
3. Alternatively, some people prefer getting many easy subjects out of the way first. That way, they feel that, numerically, they've finished most of the coursework, thereby giving themselves a psychological boost.

4. Or you could cycle through each subject. For example, a chapter from each. This can help keep you fresh. I generally tend to go with a combination of options 1 and 4.

But there's no right or wrong way here. Choose whatever works best for you from the above four. Or go ahead and make your own plan. These are just my recommendations.

Having said that, let me tell you why I chose Option 4—to study multiple subjects each day, rather than focus on just one or two subjects.

It's more effective to study multiple subjects each day, than to deep-dive into one or two subjects (Rohrer, D. 2012).

So, say, you're studying History, Physics, Chemistry and Math, it's easier to study a bit of each subject every day. This can help you learn faster than just focusing on, say, History on Monday, Physics on Tuesday, Chemistry on Wednesday and Math on Thursday.

It's easy to confuse similar information if studying a whole lot of one subject in a single day. So distribute study time for each subject, so your brain will have more time to assimilate your learning.

The second reason—mixing things up keeps it interesting.

Another reason I would recommend this method is because it ensures that every subject remains fresh in your mind at all times during the year. If you study only one subject at a time, there's a good chance that by the time you finish the other subjects and it's time for the second revision in June, the math you studied at the beginning of the year will eventually resemble Greek.

Now that we've got that out of the way, let's develop our timeline.

Note preparation and revision: April–November

Assuming that the board examinations are to be held around April or May, a year from now, we should be ready with our notes by November. We'll get to the process of how to prepare notes in a bit, but by the time winter is here (for you *Game of Thrones* fans), we should have our notes on our fingertips.

Answering questions: December–March

We're going to use the next few months—December to March—to go through questions, last years' papers, exam papers from other schools and question banks—everything we can get our hands on. Here, the goal is to practise answering questions by writing them out, and to get comfortable with the exam questions and, eventually, papers. Ideally, we want to time our answers and ensure we're comfortably within the parameters of word count and time limit. Towards the end, once you're comfortable with the writing process, you might find it faster to answer questions in your head and simply frame out the answers.

Final revision: March–April

By the time the last month comes around, you should be in a position to give any paper, any day, without any further preparation. At this stage, it's important to maintain that confidence. You've worked hard and the results will show, so it's crucial to have faith in the process. We won't be referring to any new source of information now, except the ones that we've been referring to up to this point. When you go in to give the exam, you don't want to be choosing between two sources of information in your head—that's a waste of time. It'll make you nervous and unsure, and it'll start a vicious circle that won't end well. More on this later.

So that's going to be our strategy for the next year. It's a sound strategy—nothing fancy, but extremely effective. Trust it. Trust yourself. Take a deep breath, and let's get to the process. We're good to go!

7

Step 2: The Treasure Hunt

Now that we've honed in on our strategy for the year, it's time to get into the day-to-day planning—the nitty-gritty, if you will. Our first course of action is to get our hands on as many textbooks as we can spot with the naked eye. Bring out the Hubble Telescope, if need be. Most schools have a single textbook per subject. Now, it isn't necessary that every school refer to the same book. And it most certainly isn't necessary that the board examiner—the person setting your paper or the person grading it—will refer to the same book that's currently in front of you.

Having said that, there aren't too many books within the scope of the syllabus. Generally, you'll be able to find two or three different books per subject—anything more than that is overkill.

Each textbook has its benefits. Some chapters will be better explained in one, some definitions will be more concise in the other. Another textbook might have fantastic examples. However, and this is important, by NO MEANS do you want to be remembering two versions of the same answer.

For example, let's assume Book A defines entropy as:

A thermodynamic quantity representing the unavailability of a system's thermal energy for conversion into mechanical work, often interpreted as the degree of disorder or randomness in the system.[*]

Book B, on the other hand, gives us an example and a definition. Here's what it has to say about entropy:

Let us say you have a bag of balls. You grab one ball from the bag and put it on the table. How many ways can you arrange that ball? The answer: one way. What if we grab two balls and ask the same question? Now there are more ways to arrange the two balls. We keep doing this until all the balls are on the table. At this point, there are so many ways to arrange the bag of balls that you might not even be able to count the number of ways. This situation is very much like entropy.

In this situation, entropy is defined as the number of ways a system can be arranged. The higher the entropy (meaning the more ways the system can be arranged), the more the system is disordered. Another example of this definition of entropy is

---

*https://en.oxforddictionaries.com/definition/entropy

illustrated by spraying perfume in the corner of a room. We all know what happens next. The perfume will not just stay in that corner of the room. The perfume molecules will eventually fill up the room. So the perfume went from an ordered state to a state of disorder by spreading throughout the room.[*]

If you were only referring to Book A, maybe you would never have come across the example that Book B has. Maybe the person reading your paper is more familiar with Book B, in which case the odds are that he will favour any answer that has that example. Remember, people find comfort in familiarity. Let me give you an example. We all have acquaintances in school (or life)—people who aren't really our friends but people we know of. You might not talk to them in school because you have your own group of friends and you don't feel the need to. The same goes for them, as far as you're concerned. But tomorrow, you find yourself at a function where none of your friends are around. You're alone and feeling out of place, and you can't wait to get out as soon as possible. All of a sudden, you spot that acquaintance from school and you're desperately trying to remember what his or her name is before you bump into them. Because the odds are that, surrounded by strangers, that acquaintance,

---

*https://study.com/academy/lesson/what-is-entropy-definition-law-formula.html

whatever his or her name, will quickly become your newest best friend.

Similarly, when the examiner finally sees an answer that he is familiar with, that answer will, all else remaining the same, get the highest marks. Anything else will come up short. Remember that the examiner will be grading hundreds of papers, if not more. Your job is to make it as easy for him as possible. And this is one way you're going to go about doing that.

Oh, and don't forget the entropy example. We aren't done with it just yet, and we'll be coming back to it in just a moment.

Try the horror section

I can't seem to find the calculus book in the math section

HORROR

CALCU...

LIBRARIAN

8

Step 3: The Highlighter Is Your Friend

If you were to dig up any of my 12th-grade textbooks, I'm willing to wager a fair amount that it would look more like a first grader's colouring book than a school textbook. That's because the first thing I did after I had all my textbooks in front of me was pull out the highlighter and start, well, highlighting.

Reason: Not everything in your textbook is important from the point of view of the exam.

Using a highlighter has three benefits:

1. It pushes you to read the text carefully.

2. It forces you to try to think from the point of view of the examiner.
3. It reduces the amount that you will eventually have to study. That means you have more time for less lines!

I want to dig a little deeper into Point 2.

I'm always surprised by the amount of time I see people waste on trying to assimilate every line in the book. Not only is this unnecessary, it's also extremely detrimental. Think of it this way. You have a certain amount of time to prepare for a test. And given that time frame, you also have a certain amount that your brain can retain. Does it make sense to waste that time and brainpower on parts of the textbook that can or will never be tested?

Not at all!

Ideally, you want to study only those parts that have a chance of being tested. If this isn't possible, you want to study the parts that you will be able to answer most satisfactorily, given your natural inclinations.

You have to force yourself to view the test from the point of view of an examiner. You have to think like an examiner when you read each line and ask yourself: *Is there any way I could set this as a question? Or is there any question in which this line would be used as an answer?*

You'll be surprised by how often the answer will be no. Wherever the answer is a no, forget that line.

This is primarily the difference between what they call **active reading versus passive reading.**

Characteristics of reading passively include:

- Falling off to sleep while studying.
- Hurrying through the text just to 'finish'.
- Forgetting the subject matter immediately afterwards.
- WhatsApping, Facebooking or watching the television while reading.

Characteristics of reading actively include:

- Having queries to dig out the meaning and reason behind what's written.
- Regularly taking note of the main message in your own words.
- Consistently thinking about the relationship between the text and your topic.
- Creating connections between the textbook and topics discussed in the classroom.

Active readers differ from passive readers in several ways:

Passive Reader	Active Reader
Passive readers simply read the words.	Active readers understand the reasons and ideas behind the words.
A passive reader only wants to finish as quickly as possible.	An active reader's goal is to understand and learn something.
Passive readers expect to be spoon-fed by the textbook.	Active readers are genuinely enthusiastic about learning more, and go out of their way to improve their understanding of the text.
Passive readers read mechanically, without thinking. As a result, their minds keep wandering and they cannot remember what they have read.	Active readers constantly ask critical and probing questions about each line in the text. Therefore, they are able to maintain focus and remember what they have read.

As you might have noticed, active readers are involved in the activity of reading. On the other hand, passive readers are disconnected from the reading process. There are numerous studies of reading comprehension that show increased rates of retention for students who use active reading techniques. To improve your reading comprehension, become an active reader.

Remember, the highlighter is your friend. Spend your first reading going through the chapter, and highlight anything that you feel could be important. It's possible that you won't remember too much once you've finished the chapter, but that isn't the goal for now. Do this across the textbooks that you've collected.

Here's how I would do it.

Remember that entropy example from the previous chapter? Let's take another look at it. Here it is again:

Book A defines entropy as:

A thermodynamic quantity representing the unavailability of a system's thermal energy for conversion into mechanical work, often interpreted as the degree of disorder or randomness in the system.

Book B gives us an example and a definition.

Let us say you have a bag of balls. You grab one ball from the bag and put it on the table. How many ways can you arrange that ball? The answer: one way. What if we grab two balls and ask the same question? Now there are more ways to arrange the two balls. We keep doing this until all the balls are on the table. At this point, there are so many ways to arrange the balls, you might not even be able to count the number of ways. This situation is very much like entropy.

In this situation, entropy is defined as the number of ways a system can be arranged. The higher the entropy (meaning the more ways the system can be arranged), the more the system is disordered. Another example of this definition of entropy is illustrated by spraying perfume in the corner of a room. We all know what happens next. The perfume will not just stay in that corner of the room. The perfume molecules will eventually fill up the room. So the perfume went from an ordered state to a state of disorder by spreading throughout the room.

Now, both the passages are perfectly correct. There is absolutely no sense in spending time trying to memorize both versions. That'll only confuse you. And on the day of your exam, you'll waste valuable time *choosing* the best way to frame your answer.

What you want to do is choose the best of both answers now and compile it into a single source that you'll then refer to for the rest of the year.

So, from Book A and Book B, you're going to highlight the portions that you feel combine to make up the best answer. That is, you take the best of both worlds and fuse them together to form your own definition. For example:

Entropy is defined as a thermodynamic quantity representing the unavailability of a system's thermal energy for conversion into mechanical work, often interpreted as the degree of disorder or randomness in the system. To give you an example, let us say you have a bag of balls. You grab one ball from the bag and put it on the table. How many ways can you arrange that ball? The answer: one way. What if you grab two balls and ask the same question? Now there are more ways to arrange the two balls. You keep doing this until all the balls are on the table. At this point, there are so many ways to arrange the balls that you might not even be able to count the number of ways. This situation is very much like entropy.

Now forget everything else that isn't highlighted. This way, you've made sure that you've accounted for anything that your book might have left out. Now, regardless of which book your examiner is familiar with, you've given him or her an answer that he or she has seen in some form. And I can guarantee that it'll also be a more complete answer than most of the others the examiner will read.

Remember to think from the point of view of the examiner. Keep asking yourself those two things: *Is there any way I could set this as a question? Or is there any question for which this line could be used as an answer?* You'll be surprised by how quickly you'll be able to change your style of reading. It won't take long before it starts to come naturally to you, and you won't even know that you're doing it.

Appendix 1: Are you an active reader or a passive reader?

Do you:

- Read just to get through the allocated pages and reach the end?
- Pay minimum attention to analysing the main ideas?
- Feel bored while reading?
- Feel your attention drifting?
- Avoid rereading sections or clarifying doubts to yourself?

If you've answered yes to any of these, you may be reading passively and missing opportunities to learn from the material.

Think of active reading as a discussion between yourself and the material. The process, therefore, involves repeated analysis, questioning, probing, re-examining, critiquing and developing of ideas. The advantages of active reading include:

- More effective reading and study time.
- Greater focus and attentiveness while you study.
- Increased understanding of the main information.

Appendix 2: Pull out your highlighter. Now!

You might have noticed that this chapter is a little too long, wordy, rambling, verbose… At least longer, wordier, rambling-er and verbose-er (are those even words?) than it needed to be. Try to use your highlighter to summarize this chapter to the bare essentials. See the difference.

YouTube

The reason you're failing tomorrow's test.

Inspired by www.grammarly.com

9

Step 4: Taking the Right Notes

Step 1 involved developing our strategy.
Step 2 involved collecting our sources.
Step 3 involved collating and summarizing those sources.
Step 4 involves combining those sources into a single resource.

Remember that each step has a reason:

▶   First, we want to make sure that our
    preparation leaves nothing out and that we
    provide the examiner the best possible answer.
    This requires having multiple textbooks to
    refer to. What's left out in one textbook
    might be included in another. That's why

we're spending time collecting our sources. Second, we want to make sure that our answer is familiar to the examiner. Familiarity = Comfort = Marks. That's why we're spending time collating our sources.

▸ Third, since we all have limited time and brainpower, we want to make sure we're getting the biggest bang for our buck. This involves eliminating the redundant text and highlighting only the important parts. This will ensure that we have more time to study less material—and that's exactly where we want to be, maximizing our quality of preparation.

▸ The next step is to assimilate and combine all this data into a single resource.

The act of actually taking down the notes, while definitely the longest process, is also surprisingly one of the easiest. By the time you get to the process of making your notes, you've already gone through the text once, or perhaps twice, during steps 2 and 3, and therefore have a fair idea of the concepts mentioned in the textbooks. All of a sudden, the chapter doesn't seem all that alien and daunting, which makes the process a whole lot more fun.

How to make your notes more effective

Psychologically, I found that there were a few surprisingly

innocuous tweaks that made my notes more effective:

▶ **Keep your handwriting small**

I found that keeping my handwriting small ensured that my final notes were spread across a fewer number of pages. This turned out to have a surprisingly huge impact on my psyche. Instead of having to trawl through pages and pages of unending syllabus, it seemed that I could get through a subject in no time. This gave me a psychological boost every time I had to do a revision—it didn't seem like an impossible chore.

▶ **Use different visual aids—have coloured pens, different styles for different elements**

Using different colours or styles for different elements in the textbook allowed my eye to skim through the pages much faster and more effectively. For example, I would always put a square around every definition. So whenever I would come across a black square on a page, I would know instantly that it was a definition. Similarly, whenever I was making note of an example, I would use a different-coloured pen. Over multiple revisions, I didn't waste time searching for something. If I was looking for a particular definition, I would simply skim through the black boxes. This saved me a lot of time!

▶ **Keep a uniform design scheme across all notes**
Additionally, having a uniform design scheme across my notes allowed me to picture my answer during the exams. When the exam asked for a definition, my mind would immediately picture a black box and push aside everything else.

▶ **Mouth the words while writing**
I've also found it helpful to utilize as many senses as possible when revising. There are a fair number of studies and research that indicate that people can remember material far better when multiple senses are involved. That is precisely the reason why taking notes works in the first place—it forces you to involve your hands to take notes, while using your brain to comprehend the information that your eyes are reading and then translate them into a more concise form of words and terms you understand. I found (and research by people far, far smarter than me corroborated) that mouthing the words while I made notes was one method to involve yet another sense.

Studies demonstrate that reading information out loud helps students learn faster than if reading silently (MacLeod C.M., 2010 and Ozubko, J.D., 2010).

What's the reason for this?

When you read information out loud, you not

only see it but also hear it. On the other hand, when you read your textbook silently, you only see it, hence engaging just one sense. However, it isn't practical to read every single word of every single set of notes out loud. That would take way too much time.

So here's the process I recommend:

Step 1: As you read your notes, underline the key concepts/equations. Don't stop to memorize these—underline them and move on.

Step 2: After you've completed Step 1 for the entire set of notes, go back to the underlined parts and read each key concept/equation out loud as many times as you deem necessary. Read each concept/equation slowly.

Step 3: After you've done this for each of the underlined key concepts/equations, take a three-minute break.

Step 4: When your three-minute break is over, go to each underlined concept/equation one at a time and cover it (either with your hand or a piece of paper). Test yourself to see if you've actually understood it (you can even do this once you're done making your notes and are in the revision phase).

Step 5: For the concepts/equations that you haven't successfully memorized, repeat steps 2, 3 and 4.

▶ **Err on the side of caution**

While making notes, make sure that you've left nothing out that can be tested. If anything, when unsure, err on the side of caution and include an extra line if need be. Keep your notes short, so they're quick and easy to read, but make sure that you don't lose any 'information' in the process.

▶ **Know how to expand your notes**

Make your notes in such a way that you know exactly how to expand the answer and fill in the blanks on the final day. Feel free to use shorthand, as long as it only extends to the filler words.

When I made my notes, I was confident that I didn't need to refer to anything outside of what I had written down. That is the level of confidence that you must have in them. This will, in turn, build your confidence in yourself, because they are your own notes, your own creation. All of a sudden, you'll feel like the author of the text. Maybe you've heard that the best way to learn something is to teach it? There's something similar happening here. You'll develop a sense of ownership over your notes, and hence the syllabus.

Everyone is different in the way they take similar information, assimilate it and put it together (called 'chunking' by cognitive psychologists). So while it is alright if you decide to copy your best friend's notes, try to ensure that you don't copy them verbatim. Translate your friend's notes into your own words and concepts. Failing to do so is often what prevents many students from memorizing important items.

Appendix: Please, please, please take notes by hand and not on your laptop.

Scientists recommend this, and not just because you're more likely to give in to online distractions when using your laptop. Even when laptops are used *only* for note-taking, learning is less effective (Mueller, P., 2013).

When you take notes by hand, you tend to both process and reframe the information when writing. But when you are taking notes on a laptop, the tendency is to just type in what's being said word for word without first processing it.

As such, taking notes by hand is always the smarter choice.

10

Step 5: Throw Away Your Textbooks

Yup, that's pretty much all there is to Step 5...

IT'S GOOD, BUT THE BOOK WAS BETTER

11

Revisions, Revisions, Revisions

By the time you've finished making all your notes, you'll notice that you've put on a few pounds of muscle in your writing hand, which, in all probability, will be nearly on fire and could do with a well-deserved break. Which is why the word *revision* will never elicit the same sense of relief and excitement you'll experience in that moment.

As a side benefit, you will be pretty comfortable with most of the syllabus by this point. You may not remember the notes you'd made a few months earlier, but that's perfectly fine. You'll notice that you're familiar with the concepts, and that's where we want to be at this stage.

We should now target spending the next month or two revising our notes. The first reading will be slow. Don't worry about it. It's time for us to start focusing on understanding and memorizing the definitions, examples, proofs, etc.

You'll notice that with each progressive revision, you'll start to get faster and faster. Eventually, you'll reach a point where you'll be able to identify those exact parts that you find harder than the rest. You'll find yourself skimming through the remaining syllabus and focusing on those tougher parts. Without even knowing it, you'll be shoring up your weaknesses.

Word of caution: Slow down for a second.

I should add a word of caution here. I realize that sometimes I had a tendency to rush through the parts that I found the easiest. I'd find myself thinking that since I knew a certain part, I didn't need to waste any time on it. As a result, I would be guilty of skimming through certain sections of the syllabus.

If you do this, you'll start to get rusty on the parts that you find the easiest. This is a habit that you will want to make absolutely certain that you avoid, because the sections that you find the easiest are the safety nets that will prop up your marks. Try to find a balance. Once you're comfortable with a part, devote less time to it, so that you can focus on improving the parts you find harder, but not to the extent that your main strength, becomes your weakness.

The 2:1 revision ratio

A good way to develop a balance is what I call the 2:1 ratio. For two revisions, I would focus more on my weaknesses. For the third, I would focus on everything. This ended up working quite well for me. Give it a shot and see if it works for you. You could even try changing the ratio to 3:1. Avoid anything more skewed than that.

Learn the same information in a variety of ways

Research (Willis, J., 2008) shows that different media and styles of learning stimulate different parts of the brain. The more you activate different areas of the brain, the more likely you'll be to understand and retain the information.

So to learn a specific topic, you could do the following:

- Read the notes you've made.
- Create a mind map. This basically means that you try to visualize the chapter contents solely in your head, without leaving anything out. Start from the beginning of the chapter and work your way till the end without using notes, paper or looking at the textbook for more than a second

or two. Keep track of where you get stuck, what parts you find yourself struggling with and what definitions, concepts and examples you can't remember, so that you know your weaknesses and can work on them in further revisions. Don't worry if you struggle at first. It's hard. It took me a while to get used to it. For the first few times, I could barely visualize the first page of the chapter without needing to refer to the textbook a few times. Over time, as you get more comfortable with the syllabus and with the habit of making a mind map, you realize that you can visualize the entire chapter in your head and move effortlessly through the sections without needing a pencil, paper notes or referring to the textbook. The process is superfun, and the progress you'll see yourself make will feel great. Trust me, making a mind map is as cool as it sounds. If you've seen *X-Men*, you'll feel like Professor X.

- Teach someone what you've learnt.
- Do practice problems from a variety of sources (discussed in the following chapter).

Of course, you won't be able to do all of these things in one sitting. But every now and then, when you review a topic, try to use a different resource or method—you'll learn faster that way.

Use all your senses

We all have different styles of learning and, thanks to some really cool research done by Justin Ferriman and other researchers, we now know that there are seven major ones:

1. **Visual:** Using images, videos, diagrams, colours and mind maps
2. **Physical:** Learning by doing
3. **Aural:** Using sound, rhythms, music and recordings
4. **Verbal:** Using words, both in speech and in writing
5. **Logical:** Using logic and reasoning
6. **Social:** Learning in groups or with other people
7. **Solitary:** Learning alone and through self-study

Certain ideas can seem difficult to memorize for a variety of reasons. Sometimes it could be because they are far removed from our senses, at other times because they simply don't come naturally to us. Often, when we hit a frustrating roadblock in such cases, it can help if we use our senses to come up with vivid pictures, feelings, rhymes and images that relate such information together.

We're all different in the way that we prefer to assimilate information. Since we have time on our side, it's worth experimenting at the start to identify the methods that work best for us.

For example, I avoided studying in groups, because I felt I could be far more productive studying on my own. Having said that, I would have never known the power of collaborative group discussions had I not given study groups a try. I realized that I preferred groups when it came to preparing for tests, because studying with others brought out my competitive side and pushed me to work harder. There are some people who can only study in groups, and you might never know which side of the proverbial fence you fall on if you never give it a try. Choose combinations of methods that you are most comfortable with, but to begin with, push yourself to try things that you think might be out of your comfort zone. You might surprise yourself and find a new method of studying that's far more effective than the one you've been using so far.

Connect what you're learning with something you already know

In their book *Make It Stick: The Science of Successful Learning*, scientists Henry L. Roediger III, Mark A. McDaniel and Peter C. Brown explain that the more strongly you relate new concepts to those you already understand, the faster you'll learn the new information. One way to do that is by using metaphors and analogies. These can help you easily remember material in your textbooks by comparing a complicated concept to an easy idea that you're already familiar with. When you find relationships between information, try to come up with analogies to improve your understanding.

For example, if you're learning about electricity, you could relate the flow of current to the flow of water. Voltage is similar to water pressure, current is similar to the rate of flow of water, etc.

Another example: You can think of white blood cells as 'soldiers' that defend our body against diseases, which are the 'enemies'.

When studying Physics, I would compare neurons with waves on a string. This is another way to visualize your learning.

It takes time and effort to think about how to connect new information to what you already know, but the investment is worth it. And you'll quickly become better at it to the point that it becomes effortless.

Learning is in your head

Don't be scared to get messy when scribbling out your thoughts on paper and connecting the ideas in your head. Having all these incredible-looking notes and perfectly maintained textbooks won't matter if you can't understand the information in them. Your main objective is to use them as a tool, so that you remember information not only for your exam but hopefully after that as well. Get yourself some rough registers and use them as a channel for learning, rather than as an end result.

Test your mobility

One extremely effective method to test your comprehension of a subject is to see whether you can move between concepts by linking them together. Take a rough register and try to explain the subject that you just finished studying to yourself. Quickly scribble out the main concepts in shorthand, while describing each point in your head. If you're finding it difficult to jump between sections and referencing one idea to help explain another, you will struggle to make these connections during your exams as well. Each time you do so, try to get through the chapter faster, without compromising on the level of detail, paying special attention to the parts of the chapter that you struggle with. Gradually, you'll find yourself shoring up your weaknesses in each individual chapter as you keep repeating this. Your goal should be to get through a chapter in a matter of minutes. To take it up a notch, try teaching the subject to someone else (more on this later).

Periodic review

Finally, by far the most effective tool for revision is periodic review. Periodic review is crucial if you want to move information from your short-term to your long-term memory. This will help you get better exam results. As research (Cepeda, N., 2008) shows, periodic review beats cramming hands down.

The optimal review interval varies, depending on how long you want to grasp the material that you've studied. But experience—both my own and through working with students—tells me that the following review intervals, compiled by Daniel Wong, the brilliant author of the book *The Happy Student: 5 Steps to Academic Fulfillment and Success*, work well:

- 1st review: One day after learning the new information
- 2nd review: Three days after the 1st review
- 3rd review: Seven days after the 2nd review
- 4th review: Twenty-one days after the 3rd review
- 5th review: Thirty days after the 4th review
- 6th review: Forty-five days after the 5th review
- 7th review: Sixty days after the 6th review (and so on)

12

Referring to Guides

When it comes to guides, you can either go very, very wrong (usually the case) or very, very right (hard to find). There's rarely a middle ground. My only advice when it comes to guides would be to be careful. There are a lot of poor-quality guides out there that can actually do more harm than good to your preparation.

A good guide can introduce you to new perspectives, thoughts and analyses that you may have failed to consider, which can then be added to your notes. In general, guides can be helpful for subjects like History and English, where author assessments and subjective points of view have a larger role to play in your answer.

On average, though, guides tend to be of poor

quality, and I would recommend caution when buying or referring to a guide. Close your eyes and pick up a guidebook and the odds are that it won't be a very good one.

Things to look out for when trying to identify a quality guide

There are a few surface-level checks that you can do to quickly identify or eliminate poor-quality guides right from the get-go:

Grammar

A quality guide won't have any obvious grammatical mistakes glaring right at you.

Let's eat dad.
Let's eat, dad.

Use commas.
Save a life.

Inspired by www.woodwardenglish.com

Spelling

A guide with the title 'Histry Gide' doesn't exactly scream 'buy me'. Every hair in your body should be telling you to stay away.

Topics

A comprehensive guide should cover all the topics in the syllabus and be up to date with any changes in it from the previous years. Check the chapter list of the guide and compare it with that of your textbook.

Not another textbook

A guide isn't another textbook. It should be short, crisp and concise, and should contain analyses and critiques of the syllabus, not the entire syllabus itself.

Reference

There's a good chance that a quality guide will be referenced by a teacher. Such a reference can be used as a proxy indicator for a better-quality guide.

13

Question Everything

Around December is when we should start beginning to have our syllabus on our fingertips. It's a good time to start tailoring our final preparations for the actual exam. The best way to do so, I found, was by answering questions. Answering questions helps provide a different perspective on the material that we've studied. Sometimes, we start to get used to particular patterns and flows. Questions help break those patterns and force us to look at the material from different angles and lenses. This helps shore up any cracks in our preparation that we might not have realized we had.

Decades of research have shown that self-testing is crucial if you want to improve your academic performance. In one experiment, University of Louisville psychologist Keith Lyle taught the same Statistics course to two groups of undergraduates.

For the first group, Lyle asked the students to complete a four- to six-question quiz at the end of each lecture. The quiz was based on material he'd just covered.

For the second group, Lyle didn't give the students any quizzes.

At the end of the course, Lyle discovered that the first group significantly outperformed the second on all four midterm exams.

The one key difference that separates the smartest students from the rest comes down to the questions they consistently ask themselves while learning. A smart student is driven by an insatiable curiosity to know more.

Given this, they enter each study session with three things on their mind:

1. To clarify what it is they already know.
2. To uncover what they don't know.
3. To figure out what questions they need answered.

So it isn't enough to just passively read your textbook or your notes. Study smart by quizzing yourself on the key concepts and equations. And as you prepare for your boards, do as many practice questions as you can from different sources.

Here's where the Last Ten Years' Papers come into play. The Last Ten Years' Papers, if you haven't yet chanced upon them yet, are books that, as the name suggests, contain a collection of board papers arranged chronologically. These books are available for most main subjects and contain the board-examination papers from the last ten years. Why ten years, you ask? Probably because it's a nice round number. Also, because the syllabus keeps changing every year. I think it isn't entirely unreasonable to assume that the chapter your mother studied about the workings of the *latest floppy disc* invention in her Computer Science class might have been replaced by a mildly more relevant chapter. Therefore, the older the paper, the higher the chance that the syllabus has changed multiple times since, and that the questions in the paper are no longer relevant to you. For that reason, it's quite pointless to reference questions from papers older than ten years.

Since the paper pattern in the board examinations remains fairly constant year on year, barring any major change, past papers are a great starting point to understand what kind of questions to expect. More on how to optimally analyse the Last Ten Years' Papers later.

Given their relevance, the first question books you therefore want to pick up are the Last Ten Years' Papers for each subject. These books can be purchased separately for each individual subject or, if you're really in the mood for an encyclopaedia-sized book that can double as a dumb-bell, as a compilation for all the subjects. There's also the option to buy a version with or without answers. While most of the answers in these books are sloppily written, there's no harm in referencing the answers, in case there's a point that you might not have thought of earlier. It's also worth keeping in mind that since these papers have been compiled by third parties, they often contain mistakes even in the questions. However, despite all their flaws, the Last Ten Years' Papers are a must-have in your arsenal. They are easily available in most school bookstores.

'PREPARATION FOR THE WORLD'

The good news is that the exam will be multiple choice. The bad news is that it will be in a completely different subject

(and in mandarin.

Now, a lot of people stop after going through just the Last Ten Years' Papers. They skim through the questions and think that that will be sufficient. You'll be surprised at how many people leave this to the very last moment and rush through this incredibly important period. Such a strategy will only get you so far.

So, if you can, go out and get the following:

▸ Last Ten Years' Papers (with answers, if possible) But don't stop there. Try to supplement it with:
▸ Subject-wise question banks (with answers, if possible)
▸ Other school exam papers

These three should be sufficient to provide you with more questions than you will ever need. I'd recommend that you start and end with the Last Ten Years' Papers.

Start by solving the questions on paper. For now, do not solve questions in your head, as tempted as you may be. This is important, but you may well ask, 'Why do we need to keep writing so much?'

Because, at the end of the day, you're going to be graded in a written exam.

Solving an answer in your head isn't quite the same as spending ten extra minutes solving it on paper. Yes, it's slower, but it'll lead to a marked improvement in your score.

In my 12th grade, I went for tuitions in Economics

during the summer. Our teacher would make us write each answer out in full. Questions in Economics are often subjective. By writing out each answer, we quickly started to understand how long it would take for us to solve any type of question. For example, I knew that it would take me twenty minutes to solve a 10-mark question. This ensured that I didn't spend too long on any question. I knew exactly what to write for each question prompt and didn't have to spend too much time preparing my answer in my head before writing. While writing the answer, I wouldn't have to stop, hesitate or waste time thinking about whether I was on the right track. One of the worst things that can happen while writing an answer during an exam is realizing that you have to start from the beginning because you forgot to consider an important part of the answer or misunderstood the question. This exercise also ensured that I didn't overwrite or underwrite my answer in length (this is of secondary importance).

Initially, don't worry about how long it takes you to write out the answer. It's more important to get the answer perfect—complete with definitions, explanations, examples, et al. Once you're comfortable with the writing part of it, it's time to increase the difficulty level.

Use a timer

If you can, try to solve your answers to a timer. A timer

always adds to the sense of urgency and more accurately mirrors the final experience. A ticking clock will force you to think faster and, therefore, more efficiently. From experience, I can tell you that a timer will make you nervous initially. But don't worry about it. Soon you'll stop noticing the timer altogether, and your hand will know whether it is ahead of the clock or running behind.

Pro Tip

To further increase the difficulty level, try to finish a question well before the stipulated time. Doing so increased my confidence exponentially and helped me stay relaxed on the final day, because I didn't worry about not being able to complete the paper on time—that's an unnecessary distraction—and could instead focus on answering the questions the best I could. As another benefit, I also had time for revision.

Isn't solving the Last Ten Years' Papers more than sufficient?

Not really. Don't forget to solve questions from question banks and papers that you've collected from other schools. Usually, the questions that you'll tackle here will be far more difficult than the questions you'll find in the official Last Ten Years' Papers. This will help improve your preparation and make the official questions seem relatively easier.

Pro Tip

Even if you think you know the answer to a question perfectly, don't forget to read the answer given by the guidebook, if available. While often outright wrong (beware of poor-quality guides), sometimes you'll come across a different way to answer a question. Sometimes you'll realize that you might have been misunderstanding the phrasing of a question. Such habits helped me iron out any wrinkles well before the board examinations. Now is the time to make all the mistakes and remove any misconceptions.

Why do we have to come back and re-solve the Last Ten Years' Papers? Isn't that a waste of time?

Towards the end of your preparation, come back to the Last Ten Years' Papers for a final revision. By now you'll be ready for the exam on every possible front and the questions in front of you should be a cakewalk. You don't want to spend more time writing out any more answers. Spend this time going through the questions in your head and understanding the patterns.

But most importantly, come back to the Last Ten Years' Papers for a psychological boost. Now isn't the time to learn anything new. It's far more important to get your confidence as high as possible. Because you'll already have solved these questions a few months ago, you'll be able to solve all the questions without any trouble the second time around. You'll feel good going into the exam and this will, in turn, allow you to give your paper with a cool head, minimizing nerves and maximizing potential. More importantly, you'll be getting accustomed to the official exam language and question types one final time.

Only in math class can you buy 100 bananas and no one asks you what the hell is wrong with you.

14

Flash Cards

Flash cards are awesome. Period. Use them. Overuse them. Then use them some more.

Why we need a change up

The one problem with revising your notes over and over again is that your brain gets used to the order of the text. And sometimes that lulls you into a false sense of security. You think that you're on top of your syllabus when in fact you're not—you're just comfortable with the order in which you've been revising your syllabus. But all of a sudden, if you disrupt that order, you'll find yourself in disarray. That's why answering questions is so crucial. It breaks that linear flow that you've developed, reading the same notes over and over again in the same order each time.

One way to improve the quality of your revision is to change that order. Start from a random chapter and work your way through the notes in an order that your eyes aren't accustomed to. It's a small tweak that yields a big dividend.

Another way to take it further is the use of flash cards.

What are flash cards?

For those of you who don't know, a flash card is a learning aid that contains a small amount of information on two sides.

On one side you write the topic (say, *Entropy*) or the question (say, *Example of entropy*), and on the other, you write the definition of the topic or the answer to whatever question is being asked. You shuffle them and pull one out at random, read the prompt and answer the question. If you get it right, you put the card in the 'right' pile; if you get it wrong, you put it in the 'wrong' pile. After you are done, you can start with the wrong pile. The ones you get right this time are shifted to the 'right' pile, until there are no more cards left in the 'wrong' pile.

When I was preparing for the boards, I made physical flash cards—which took a while. But now you can just download a flash card app on your phone, and it'll do most of the work for you. If you mark a question as incorrect (you answered it wrong), the app will throw it back to you after some time and continue to do so till you get everything right.

What are the benefits of flash cards?

With flash cards, the order in which you recall information is completely out of your control, and the randomness significantly improves the quality of your preparation by disrupting any rhythm that you may have developed over time. Some apps will also save statistics such as which flash cards you consistently get wrong, so that you can target them in future.

That this revision process is more like a 'game' also makes it more fun. I typically found this to be a great way to end my day. It was almost like a quick recap. You'll be surprised at how quickly you can go through a full bunch of flash cards.

When should you make flash cards?

One thing I used to do was add anything that I got wrong to a flash card. Any definition that I found particularly hard, or any date I couldn't remember got added to the pile immediately. Try to do the same—whenever you come across something difficult, add it immediately to your flash card app.

When should you revise your flash cards?

I would revise the most difficult concepts with the flash cards every night before sleeping. It's a great way to reinforce the learning in a quick, fun and engaging manner.

Ideal time to use flash cards: Fifteen minutes before you go to sleep

Recommended apps: Cram and Brainscape

It's never too late to learn something ~~stupi~~...new.

15

Throw in the Specifics

So far we've discussed ways to improve our preparation. I'd now like to discuss small tweaks that can help improve our answers. One such tweak is surprisingly simple—throw in some numbers, details or specifics.

While I was preparing, I would make it a point to make a note of certain details that I was sure would help my answer stand out—things like **dates, names, numbers** or anything else that would make my answer more specific. I would always try to add specific details to my answer that would make it stand out among the rest.

Now, I realized very early on that no one can remember every number, date or name that appears in every textbook on every subject. It's pointless to even try.

I also realized that I wasn't very good at remembering dates and other similar details. So, in my notes, I would list out the essential details and highlight them, leaving out any I felt would confuse me (unless they were extremely important to remember). I had to make a conscious effort to remember these specifics and details, but because I had identified this as a weakness in me, I paid special attention to it.

Have a look at the following examples and try to decide which one reads better.

Textbook

Indian Railways is the fourth-largest railway network in the world, comprising 119,630 kilometres of total track with 7,216 stations at the end of 2015–16. In 2015–16, Indian Railway carried 8.107 billion passengers annually, or more than 22 million passengers a day, and 1.101 billion tons of freight annually. It is the world's eighth-biggest employer and had 1.331 million employees at the end of 2015–16. In 2015–2016 Indian Railways had revenues of ₹1.683 trillion. It is divided into 17 zones, which are further subdivided into divisions.

Question: Tell us about the Indian Railways.

Answer 1:

Indian Railways is the fourth-largest network comprising many stations. It carries billions of passengers and billions of tons of freight annually. Indian Railways is the world's eighth-biggest employer, employing millions of people. It also earns trillions in revenue. It is a complex system that is divided into many zones and subdivisions.

Answer 2:

Indian Railways is the fourth-largest network, comprising in excess of 7,000 stations spread over 119,000 kilometres of tracks as of 2015–16. It carries 8.1 billion passengers and 1.1 billion tons of freight annually. Indian Railways is the world's eighth-biggest employer, employing more than 1.3 million Indians as of 2015–16, when it earned approximately ₹1.5 trillion in revenue. It is a complex system that is divided into 17 zones that are further subdivided into divisions.

Which answer do you think will fetch more marks?

Both answers are correct. But Answer 1 just doesn't have the specifics that Answer 2 does. Most answers presented to the examiner will be similar to Answer 1. The ones who have made the effort to present the details provided in Answer 2 will be rewarded with a far better grade.

Look at some simple tricks that I used above to add the level of specificity without too much effort:

1. Rounding off the numbers

I realized there was no way I was going to remember

a number like 119,630 or 7,216. I probably wouldn't even need to—the examiner wouldn't be looking for that kind of detail and the odds were that he wouldn't even know the exact number. In fact, I was willing to bet that the exact number would differ from book to book. So remembering the exact number to me was just a waste of time. I just needed to make sure that I provided enough detail to distinguish my answer from the rest of the pile. So I rounded off the numbers and made it easier for myself.

2. **Finding patterns that you can memorize**

   I removed some decimal places by converting 8.107 to 8.1, and 1.101 to 1.1. I could have even used 8 and 1, but here I noticed a pattern that would, in fact, help me remember the data. Both figures ended in .1, and I made a note of that.

3. **Throwing in the easy details**

   I made sure that I included the easy details, such as '2015–16'. Leaving out a detail that simple doesn't make sense anyway.

4. **Using approximations**

   Note that I changed ₹1.7 trillion in revenue to ₹1.5 trillion. It could be that I forgot the exact figure, so I chose to use the closest round figure that would still be accurate. 1.5 is an easier number to remember than 1.7.

If you notice, there are still details that I've left out in my answer, compared to the text. But nobody expects you to reproduce every detail in the textbook. My answer is more than sufficient to get me that perfect score.

> **TIP:**
> If you like, you can even make these minor adjustments in your notes.

Use memory games (mnemonic devices)

Memory games, or mnemonic devices, are means of remembering information using simple word associations. Most often, people string together words to form a nonsensical sentence that is easy to remember. The first letter of each word can then be used to stand for something else—the piece of information you're trying to remember. For example, a common mnemonic example is 'Please Excuse My Dear Aunt Sally'. If we string together the first letter of every word, we get PEMDAS—Parentheses, Exponents, Multiply, Divide, Add, Subtract—the order we need to follow to solve one of those overcomplicated math equations that we all love so much.

Another example: When I found myself struggling to remember ion flow in Chemistry, I used the following mnemonic that saved my life on more than one occasion, and even gave me a good chuckle every time!

- **Red cat:** *Reduction at cathode*
- **An ox:** *Anode for oxidation*
  The words *anode* and *oxidation*, both begin with vowels. Also, both *reduction* and *cathode begin with consonants*
- **Fat cat:** Electrons flow **F**rom **A**node **T**o **Cat**hode

Using mnemonic devices like acronyms has been proven to increase learning efficiency. In addition, you could summarize the information into a comparison table, diagram or mind map. These tools will help you learn the information much faster.

Mnemonic devices are helpful because you use more of your brain to remember visual and active images than you do to remember just a list of items. Using more of your brain means better memory. The key to such memory devices is that the new phrase or sentence you come up with has to be more memorable and easier to remember than the information you're trying to learn. Having said that, mnemonics don't work for everyone. So if they don't work for you, don't stress—simply don't use them.

Etc.
*The abbreviation I use in my answer when
I can't think of any other examples*

Inspired by www.grammarly.com

16

Answer Structure Your

In the words of the fictional Jedi master Yoda, 'Write an answer like this, and no marks receive shall you.'

Think otherwise, do you?

In the same way that a sentence must be constructed properly, so must the answer to any question. You could argue, however, that despite Yoda's questionable sentence construction and grammar, he was able to convey the message that he wished to. After all, you did understand what he was trying to say, didn't you?

While that might be true, it doesn't change the fact that there was a far more efficient way for Yoda to convey his message, if only he had decided to pay a little more attention in English class, instead of skipping lectures to slay bad guys and heckle R2 droids.

The same analogy applies to the answer structure. Two answers with the exact same content but different structures can have widely different impacts on the reader. I realized this when I was reading an answer that my brother had written. Two years younger than me, Rishi was preparing for his 10th boards when I was preparing for my 12th. He wanted to know why he had got a terrible grade on an answer that he, in his opinion, had solved extremely well. He had listed out all the facts, he'd given the required examples, he'd taken an extra sheet and basically checked every box off the frontbencher's 'how to ace a test' checklist. All in all, he had walked out of the exam hall thinking that he had finally nailed a test and, for a change, wouldn't have to listen to mum's obligatory lectures on a career in McDonald's if he kept walking the same path. He was expecting a solid grade and was thrilled.

He was a little less thrilled, though, when he saw a 50 per cent stamped across his answer sheet and realized that the prospect of mum's lecture—which had, for an ephemeral moment, faded into oblivion—had come swelling back in a crescendo that sounded like Hans Zimmer had fallen asleep on his organ. More than being annoyed, he was frustrated, because he couldn't seem to figure out what on earth was wrong with his answer!

So, like all younger siblings, as a last resort, he trudged up to his 'suddenly far wiser' elder brother for advice—a rare moment of deference that suited his convenience. I wasn't complaining, though. It gave me the equally rare opportunity to make him go through the rounds of obligatory grovelling before magnanimously deciding to grant him audience.

I went through his answer, and it took me all of five minutes to figure out what was wrong with it, because I couldn't find what was *right* with it. The answer was so long, unwieldy and verbose that anything *right* with the answer was lost in the ocean of verbal extravagance that lay before me. It took me several detailed reads to understand his answer and accept his claim that he had indeed included everything that needed to be included.

But we won't have the luxury of a loving elder brother to scrutinize our answers with a fine-toothed comb in our board answer papers. Our goal is not only to include all the necessary details in our answers but to ensure that the important bits—the *money sentences,* if you will—jump out at the person reading it.

How do we go about doing that?

Structure!

As I've mentioned before, it's our job to make the examiner's life as easy as possible. And one way we're going to manage that is by structuring our answer in the best possible way.

(Note: This is applicable to the slightly longer, more subjective answers.)

1. Use an introduction, but keep it short and crisp

You've probably heard the sayings 'the first impression is the last impression' or the slightly more mushy 'love at first sight'. The first paragraph of your answer is your chance to make a good impression—to grab the examiner's attention and make him or her want to read your answer further. Or at least show him or her that you know what you're talking about. A good first paragraph is crucial if you want to convince your examiner that your ideas are worthy of his or her time and attention. Introductions are important because they not only provide a first impression, but also establish credibility with your examiner.

However, the introduction isn't where you're going to get your main marks in a board-examination answer, so you shouldn't waste too much time or space on it. Doing so will detract from your answer and bury the main points that will fetch you marks. A long, rambling introduction can also convey the message that you're just filling up space on the answer sheet. On the other hand, not having an introduction can make the answer seem unorganized and rushed.

In short, an introduction won't fetch you marks but it can cost you some. If I were forced to choose, I would rather have an answer that has no introduction but gets straight to the money points, than a long, verbose one that buries the main points and makes the examiner lose interest in what he or she is reading. A short, crisp few lines should ideally be your introduction, which should have five important responsibilities: get the examiner's attention, introduce the topic, explain its relevance to the examiner, state a thesis or a purpose, and outline the main points.

Your job here is to convince the examiner that:

▶ Your answer is organized and well laid out, and that you know what you are writing about.

▶ You aren't just faffing, gobbling up space, writing a few extra lines, beating around the bush and repeating the same information a few phrases later, with no substance to show for it. So keep it short and sweet.

▶ The rest of your answer will be exactly what he is looking for and will, in all probability, cover what is required. You can do this by introducing the money points in a sentence or two.

2. Get to the money points ASAP

Think about it—why do movie channels like HBO save their main movies for the 9 p.m. slot? Why do sports events schedule their marquee events on weekends? Why do they call it 'prime time'? Because that's when the audience is at its hungriest for entertainment. You want to ensure that you save the best possible entertainment for that slot, so you can wow your audience. Similarly, your money points are those parts of your answer that will fetch you the bulk of your marks. Your 'prime time' slot is at the beginning of the answer, right after the two to three lines of introduction. This is when the examiner's attention is at its peak. Put the money points up front, right after the introduction, so that it catches his attention.

Your job is to capitalize on this and ensure that he or she realizes that you know your facts.

3. Give your money points the maximum airtime

It goes without saying that your money points are what you should be spending most of our time on. There's no point if the 9 p.m. movie gets over in ten minutes, is there? As an audience member, I'd feel cheated. Make sure that you devote most of your time developing the main point of your answer.

4. Descend the ladder of importance

Your points should be organized in descending order

of importance. That is, the most important point comes first and the least important comes last, coinciding with the ebb in the examiner's attention.

5. Use visual cues to highlight your money points

You have to ensure that your main points jump out at the examiner. By no means should he or she have to search your answer for these points. One way to make sure of that is to use visual cues. These could include the use of:

▸ Different-coloured pens to indicate a heading, or the start of a new point.
▸ Underlines, bold letters, etc.
▸ Paragraphs to indicate the start of a new point.
▸ Bullet points to make the answer easier to read.

Now, bullet points are a source of contention in the exam world. Some people swear by them—bullet points make the answer more concise and easier to read. They can also seamlessly facilitate the introduction of a new point. On the other hand, conservative examiners frown upon the use of bullet points. My advice is that it's safe to use bullet points in mathematical subjects such as Physics, Chemistry, Biology, Economics, etc. But it's safer to avoid them in subjects such as English, where you're going to be judged on proper grammar, which isn't the case in mathematical subjects. In fact, I'd go so far as to say that mathematical-subject examiners might actually prefer summarized bullet points over long, verbose answers. In the case of subjects such as History and Geography, I feel it depends upon the answer. In most cases, bullet points should be fine, but I wouldn't overuse them here. **Your job:** Ensure that the money points jump out at the reader without any effort on his or her part.

6. A conclusion

Just like an introduction, a conclusion might not fetch you marks, but it sure can cost you that perfect score. I would go so far as to say that a conclusion might actually be more important than the last few points of your answer. If you've followed this book, since we're descending the ladder of importance, the last few points will be the least important points of your answer. Since the examiner has already read the money points at the beginning of the answer, there is a good chance that he or she feels that you know what you are writing about and skims through the bottom part of your answer. He or she will, however, read the last paragraph—of that you can be certain.

Use the conclusion to wrap up your answer. It doesn't need to be more than a line or two. Remember, the examiner has probably already mentally decided upon the marks to give you. The lack of a conclusion might indicate that you didn't have the time to finish the answer. It can make your perfect answer seem rushed, for which you might get penalized. Avoid that by rounding off your answer.

Your job: Seal the deal.

17

Recharge Your Batteries

As a child, I would dream that I'd become the greatest guitarist in the world someday. I picked up a guitar when I was ten and was only fourteen when I stepped into the tiny sound booth of a rundown studio for the first time. I was always passionate about music. While preparing for my board exams, I would make it a point not to give up on my hobbies, be it pretending to be Jimi Hendrix on the guitar or unsuccessfully emulating Roger Federer on the tennis court. It helped me stay refreshed—it was almost like a reset button. It kept me alert and mentally relaxed.

But don't overdo it

At the same time, I would make sure that I wasn't overdoing it. This wasn't the year for me to become an expert tennis player or musician. There's enough time for those exploits when the exams are over. I would strongly recommend that you continue pursuing your hobby, but in moderation. An hour or two a day spent on doing something that revitalizes you is time well spent.

'Yes, mom. Of course I'm studying. I'm on a course.'

Get the balance right

This might sound obvious, but you'll be surprised at how many people fail to get the balance right. A lot of people see it as a complete waste of time, while others end up getting too distracted by their own hobbies and losing sight of their priorities for the year. Getting the right balance is crucial.

So spend an hour or two playing video games, watching your favourite television show or playing cricket—whatever it is that you enjoy doing. It doesn't matter if it's indoors or outdoors. I've noticed a lot of parents say that it's essential to spend time outdoors. For different reasons, absolutely! But for our purposes, it doesn't matter whether you can make it to the moon and back in your free time, as long as it recharges your batteries. When you get back to your study table, you should be raring to go.

Time advised: About two hours per day

18

Study in Small Chunks

'*Oh, you know, I spend ten hours studying every day. You only study for four hours? Bro, you're never going to manage...*'

I've noticed that a lot of people treat the time spent 'studying' as gospel. They equate time spent at the desk—regardless of the quality of the input or the output—with effort, and expect corresponding results to go with it.

These are the people who'll brag about the number of hours they spend studying every day and try to compete on parameters that have little direct consequence on exam results.

Ask yourself—do you do the same? Be honest.

In all likelihood, the answer will be yes. I know, because I was guilty of this for a long time as well. I thought that the more hours I spent staring at my book, the higher my grade would be. Before a test, I'd meet my friends and we'd try to one-up each other on who had studied the longest, or who had stayed up at night the latest. I would get nervous when I realized that my classmates had stayed' up later than me. I would think there was no way I could ever beat them in any test or examination. So even before the exam had started, I had lost the fight because of my defeatist attitude.

It took me a while to realize that no one from that group ended up scoring consistently well in tests over a period of time. Not even close. They did well, sure, and sometimes did really well, but it was usually a one-off—occasions that were few and far between. When I looked at their results over a sustained period of time, their results weren't anything to write home about.

And then there was this one kid, well on his way to becoming the school captain of our batch. He was involved in debates, sports, extracurriculars— you name it. You'd look at him and wonder if he even had a minute to open his book. Surely, there had to be a trade-off. He had to be sacrificing his academic results, I thought! He even had a great social life! There was no humanly fathomable way he could be acing any test, except, perhaps, from the bottom.

And then the test results came—and there he was, at the top of the class.

'Probably a fluke, lucky bastard,' I thought to myself and wrote it off to fortuitous luck. There's no way a guy who had studied half the amount I had could get twice my grade without sheer luck.

And then the same thing happened in the next test—and the next and the next and the next...

There comes a time when even the most cynical of us have to stop attributing everything to Lady Luck and acknowledge that maybe, just maybe, the guy isn't a walking, talking barrel of fortune bracelets.

Like all adroit problem-solvers (I guess I was destined to become a problem-solving, jet-setting management consultant from an early age), I decided to get to the bottom of this. After many hours spent stalking the guy— in retrospect, a simple question would have sufficed (he was a gem of a person)—I realized that the secret lay in the *way* he studied, not in *how much*.

Difference No. 1: Focus only on yourself and your preparation. Stop comparing yourself to others.

I realized that he was never part of the group that discussed how long they had studied, or which revision they were on. He didn't care or allow it to affect him one bit.

Difference No. 2: Study smart, and study effectively. Don't study long.

Though he studied less, he made every revision count. He did so by studying effectively—by paying attention in class when the rest of us were busy dozing off or making fun of our teachers; taking effective notes; and genuinely understanding the syllabus, as opposed to blindly memorizing it.

Once I understood his method, there was no looking back. I incorporated these simple attitude changes in the way I studied and noticed a dramatic improvement in my results. And these are the simple tweaks that I'm sharing in this book—tweaks that will help you maximize your potential.

Anyway, back to the question: If you are guilty of the same habit that I once was—focusing on quantity instead of quality—change it. Without exception, such an attitude will never get you where you want to be, because you're focusing on the wrong things.

▶ Stop focusing on the number of hours you spend studying. It isn't going to get the attention of that girl you like. At best, you'll get slapped with a 'nerd' label across your forehead.

▶ Stop trying to study for hours at a stretch.

▶ Stop worrying about how much your friends have studied. And don't be party to any discussion that involves hours. It's a waste of time. Remember, the grass always looks greener on the other side. Such discussions will only fill you with self-doubt. Before an exam, you need to be feeling as confident as possible.

▶ Twenty minutes spent studying effectively—if you incorporate the methods detailed in this book, you will be studying effectively—and twenty minutes spent taking a break beat sixty minutes spent just staring at the book. Hands down.

▶ Most importantly, trust in our process.

Remember, quality always, always, always trumps quantity.

Revision

The art of watching a movie, browsing Facebook and eating popcorn with your Physics textbook lying close by.

Inspired by www.grammarly.com

So how should we study (with regard to time—the chapter assumes that by incorporating the other tweaks detailed in this book, you are studying effectively)?

In the same vein as the previous chapter, I find that I study best in small intervals. I almost never study for more than twenty to forty minutes at a stretch. I've found that after that period, my attention starts drifting and I don't end up giving it my 100 per cent. In fact, there are numerous scientific studies to prove that studying in small intervals is a more effective way of studying than sitting for longer hours at a stretch with a book.

It's human nature to avoid studying, because most of us view it as a chore or a task. If, however, you can come up with rewards to make the study process more fun, while simultaneously reinforcing what you're doing, you may be pleasantly surprised by the change you find in your attitude towards studying over time.

Start by breaking up your study time into small, manageable segments. Think about it—does studying for four hours at a time with no breaks sound like fun? Neither is it fun, nor is it realistic for most people.

So here's what I suggest:

▶ Study for 20–40 minutes
▶ Take a break for 10 minutes

You'll find that this way, not only is studying more sustainable and enjoyable, but also much more productive. When you enjoy what you're doing, you automatically end up doing a better job of it.

How do we accomplish this?

Divide study time into segments that work for you. If you have to digest a whole textbook chapter, find sections in the chapter and commit to reading and taking notes for one section at a time. Maybe you only do one section in a sitting, maybe you do two. Find the limits that seem to work for you.

The moment you find your attention wandering, it's time to get up from the chair. If you aren't giving it your 100 per cent, there's no point. It's far better to spend 20 minutes studying and 10 minutes relaxing than to spend 40 minutes blankly staring at your book and not retaining anything. As mentioned in the above chapters, 20 minutes spent in 'active' reading is far more useful than 40 minutes spent in 'passive' reading.

Set targets and reward yourself if you meet them

If you succeed in your goals (such as doing two sections of a chapter in one sitting), give yourself a real reward. Perhaps it's saying 'I'll treat myself to some good dessert tonight at dinner' or 'I'll watch an episode of *Game of Thrones*' or 'I can spend an extra 30 minutes gaming for every two sections of a book chapter I read'. The point is to find a reward that is small but real—and to stick to it. By setting these limits on your behaviour, you're teaching yourself discipline, which will be a handy skill to have throughout your life.

19

Find Someone to Lecture

You may have come across the 'teaching is the best way to learn' quote at some point in life. I prefer the less colloquial but similarly intentioned, 'Teaching is nature's way of letting you know how terrible your understanding really is.'

One fine day, for some reason, Rishi decided that it was in humanity's best interest for him to volunteer to help his math tuition teacher with her workload. For some inexplicable reason, she concurred with his worldview and took him up on his offer.

Now, my younger brother was always a smart chap, but by no dictionary definition of the word could he (at the time) be considered '*smart enough to teach someone*'.

It didn't take long for his tuition teacher to regret her decision. In less than twenty-four hours, she got the fright of her life when she heard chants of '*Oh Captain, My Captain*' from her tuition room and raced to see which of her students was in dire need of a gift card for a lobotomy.

Imagine the poor lady's horror when she walked into the room to find Rishi standing atop two desks, straddling them like a poor man's Colossus of Rhodes, surrounded by sixteen-years-olds held in captive awe, in a scene that would have made Robin Williams proud.

Rishi was clearly taking his new role of teaching assistant extremely seriously.

The comedy of it all aside, back home, we all noticed a marked and immediate difference in Rishi's own results in math. All of a sudden, his grades were higher and the feedback from his own teachers indicated a significant increase in classroom engagement on his part. More than anything, he seemed to be genuinely enjoying studying math—which we had so far thought impossible.

You may think you understand a topic, but it's not until you've tried (and repeatedly failed) to explain it to someone who doesn't understand your made-up terminology and rules of thumb that you realize what you really know and what you just pretend to understand.

For a long time now, people have theorized that the best way to learn something is to try to teach it to someone else. *'While we teach, we learn,'* said the Roman philosopher Seneca.

So why is teaching such an effective way to learn?

1. It inculcates a sense of responsibility

According to journalist and writer Annie Murphy Paul, teaching provides a sense of accomplishment and purpose. Researchers have found that students enlisted to tutor others put in more effort to understand the material, remember it more precisely and apply it more effectively. In fact, student teachers score higher on tests than pupils who are learning only for their own sake. This has been dubbed 'the protégé effect' by many scientists.

2. It forces you to be thorough

More importantly, teaching others helps you get a better handle on the material. Since you have to sort out the material and get it straight, you end up struggling with the material until it's crystal clear in your own head—because only then will it be clear enough for your students to understand.

3. It helps you identify the areas that you actually thought you understood but didn't

It's only after you've been repeatedly plundered with questions on topics you thought you had on your fingertips that you identify which ones you indeed understand and which ones you don't.

4. It forces you to succinctly present your points of view

There's no better way to realize that your long, convoluted and rambling answer is terrible than to watch your best friends (and in this case, students) doze off in front of you. To grab your students' attention, you need to explain your topic effectively. Being concise plays a big role in achieving that goal. This will benefit your written answer as well.

5. It strips you of terminology

You: *The second law of thermodynamics states that an isolated system's entropy never decreases.*

Student: *What's entropy?*

You: *(Realizing that you have no clue whatsoever, because you simply memorized the book's definition and came to teach this class) Why don't you think about it and give me an answer?*

(While simultaneously searching your textbook, Wikipedia, Google, praying to God—anything that works, really—for the answer. Your student, in the meantime, rambles incoherently about the topic and you put yourself on the back for impressively turning the situation on its head with surprising alacrity.)

Student: *(Continuing to ramble, demonstrating his remarkable proficiency at inventing new definitions of 'entropy'.)*

You: *(Relieved and now pretending to be wise, having finally found the answer and, along with it, your recently violated sense of composure) Entropy is a thermodynamic quantity representing the unavailability of a system's thermal energy for conversion into mechanical energy, often interpreted as the degree of disorder or randomness in the system.*

Student: *(Blank expression, unsure where to even begin) What's mechanical energy? What's a system?*

You: *You know what, let's treat that as homework for today.*

(Tomorrow, after you've actually understood the terms yourself.)

You: *Alright, everyone pull out your earphones. Have you ever wondered why your earphones always come out in a bunch of knots, no matter how careful you were when you put them in your pocket?*

Your favourite daily ritual of having to untangle them has nothing to do with your earphones having a sadistic desire to ensure that your day gets off to the most miserable start. Your earphones are tangling themselves on purpose. It's just that, while there is one way for them to be 'ordered' (i.e., untangled), there are probably infinite ways for them to stay tangled. Therefore, the probability of them remaining untangled is minuscule compared to the probability of your earphones keeping you in a state of knots yourself. That's entropy for you. Entropy is basically chaos—the lack of order or predictability.

Oh, and mechanical energy is the energy in an object due to its motion or position. And a system is just a bunch of different things that can together do stuff that no single 'thing' can do on its own.

You know you've understood a concept well if you can explain it to a layman in simple sentences without the use of complex terminology.

6. It forces you to answer questions

Sometimes it's easier to ask questions that test the granularity of your understanding in a verbal discussion, as highlighted above. Which is why an oral conversation will force you to answer questions that seem too obvious to ask in a written exam. Which leads us to...

7. It shores up holes in your understanding

For this reason, teaching others improves your understanding of concepts in a far more detailed manner.

20

When to Study?

What is the best time to study? It's one of those endless debates among students—is it better to study at night or during the day? Each side has its loyal advocates, who will speak at length about the advantages of their preferred method to try and convince you of the benefits of their choice.

Therefore, it's no surprise that I'm often asked what the best time to study is or what time I preferred studying in (for the record, I'm more of a night owl—I preferred studying at night, although, of course, during my 12th grade, I had to study through the day as well, as probably—though not necessarily—will you. More on this later in the chapter).

To be honest, on a scale of 1 to 10, 10 being the most important factor for our results, the '*best time to study*' would be a lowly 2 or 3 in my opinion. I believe that there were other things that I did (or purposely didn't do) that had a far greater impact on my result than did the '*time at which I studied*'. If for nothing else, then simply because in your 12th grade, you will be studying a whole lot! For that reason, which part of the twenty-four hours you spend studying becomes a tad irrelevant, if you're studying as much as you need to.

I think it's, therefore, more important to look at:

▶ What part of the year we are currently in
▶ Whether there is a particular time when we can study a particular subject more effectively

Let's see if there are small changes we can make that will have an incremental improvement on our results.

Let's look at the first point—what part of the year we are currently in.

During school term, you'll have to wake up early to attend classes. By no means would I recommend skipping your classes. I doubt your parents would either. For that reason, it becomes virtually impossible to study late into the night. Staying up late can keep you drowsy at school the next day, and you will not be able to concentrate on what is being taught. So, even if you are a night person, plan your night-study schedule well and have a cut-off time for bed. Whether you like it or not, you *have* to study during the time you have available, which is from afternoon, when you return from school, till perhaps 11 or 12 at night. That's your study window. Alternatively, you have the option of waking up early and studying before you get ready for school, in which case you'll end up sleeping early. Either case, your window remains the same. (In another chapter, I'll discuss how we can get the most out of time spent in class.)

During the summer, winter and pre-board-examination study breaks, however, we have a larger window to spread our self-studies across. So, is there a particular time when we can study a particular subject or concept more effectively?

What do scientists say?

Dr Jane Oakhill, a professor of Psychology at the University of Sussex, conducted a number of experiments to determine how our memory is affected by the time of day. It turns out we process two types of memory—declarative and semantic—differently throughout the day.

In the morning, we tend to be better at declarative memory tasks—which is our ability to recall exact details, like names, places, dates and facts. However, in the early evening, our brain is better at semantic memory tasks—our ability to integrate new information with what we already know, and make it meaningful.

Here are a few things that will help us in our studies:

1. In the morning (till lunch time):

    ▶ We tend to be better at tasks that rely on our ability to recall exact details, like names, places, dates and facts.

    ▶ Scientific studies have shown that the early hours of the day are the best time for our analytical brain to perform the most complex tasks (like reading, comprehension, application and repetition).

    ▶ For this reason, some scientists call this time of day the brain's peak performance time— roughly two to four hours after we wake up. Visual memory is considered to be better in the morning and critical thinking around noon, so plan learning activities accordingly.

2. Most people, however, go through a 'slump' in the afternoon, between 1 p.m. and 4 p.m., and should take this time to relax.

3. In the early evening (4 p.m. to 7 p.m.), our brain is better at tasks that require our ability to integrate new information with what we already know, and make it meaningful.

4. The creative part of the brain works actively at night before you go to bed.

Okay, that's all great. But what does that mean for me?

Putting all this together, when you're planning out your day, you want to:

▶ Study new material earlier in the day.
▶ Use the early evening to integrate new knowledge into what you already know.

Thus, the morning is best for researching information, while the early evening is better for synthesizing and applying it.

Here's how I structured my day, and could be one way you could structure yours too.

This is a sample breakdown of how you might want to go about it for the best results:

Early morning

I'm not a morning person and never have been. I prefer waking up late, studying later in the day and sleeping quite late. I'm much more efficient and alert at night, so whenever I have a choice, this is the pattern I follow. However, in the 12th grade, I knew that I'd have to put in some extra hours to get the results I wanted. So, despite hating to wake up early, I increased the length of my day by pushing myself to be the first in our fairly active house to get out of bed.

5 a.m.–7 a.m.: Every morning I'd wake up around 5 and use this time to revise my notes and solve questions in my head. Answering questions in your head forces you to visualize the answer, and if done properly, can stimulate a very different response in your mind from writing an answer out on paper. The important bit is to make sure you force yourself to answer the question completely and avoid resorting to the tendency to skip parts of the answer you think you might know. It also helps you to 'see' the answer and connect the various parts in your head at the same time, without the aid of paper and pen.

Since all I needed was just a book in my hands, I could stay in bed, all snuggled up in a blanket. Because it was cold, I'd make myself a cup of hot chocolate with marshmallows—a treat I'd grown up fantasizing about, having been brought up on a steady diet of Enid Blyton books, where the characters would sip cups of hot cocoa around a warm fire on a chilly moonlit night.

All of a sudden, waking up early in the morning didn't feel like much of an effort—in fact, I often looked forward to it, because early mornings meant scampering around an empty house to rustle up my early-morning treat. Instead of being my least favourite thing in the world, waking up early became the most exciting part of the day. Literally.

I avoided taking notes early in the morning. Making

notes would have entailed getting out of bed and studying on a table and chair, in a far less snuggly environment. While it's possible that making notes on a table might have been more productive than revising in bed, where I was admittedly guilty of dozing off a few times, I stuck with it. The reason was that if I disliked waking up too much, there was a good chance that I would stop waking up early altogether.

For me, the decision was between waking up (and working at 80 per cent efficiency) versus not waking up at all (and losing those hours = 0 per cent efficiency). I decided to go with Option No. 1, primarily because I found a way to make waking up early, an activity I hated, into one that I actually looked forward to, with a few small tweaks! Looking at the bigger picture, that's the compromise I made, and it seems to have worked for me. I'd strongly recommend that you find ways to take activities that you find yourself struggling with, and figure out creative tweaks to make them fun. You'll be surprised at how effective the smallest of changes can be. As long as you find a way to enjoy what you do, you'll stick with it. And not just that, you'll do it well. Win win.

Morning

8 a.m.–1 p.m.: This is the best time of the day for test review, problem-solving, report-writing and math-oriented work.

Afternoon

1 p.m.–4 p.m.: This is the best time for movement-oriented tasks, like filing away homework and assignments, running errands, practising music and art, or simply taking some well-deserved rest. Most people suffer a 'slump' during this period. I used this time to play tennis or the guitar, or just sleep.

I love homework. I sit and stare at it for hours.

Early evening

4 p.m.–7 p.m.: This is the best time of day for undertaking reading-heavy tasks, like studying English Literature or History, or anything that involves long passages.

Night

It is true that things look different at night. The night **can increase your creative efficacy** and help you see concepts differently. And since the rest of the house is asleep and can't disturb you, it is a peaceful and quiet time, when it's just you and your books. There are no distractions—except perhaps the bed. Most of your friends are asleep and your social networks will be less active. The mind's creative output increases at night—maybe that's why so many of us writers, poets and artists work until the wee hours of the morning.

9 p.m.–2 a.m.: I used this as my main study time. Everything revolved around this period. I was mentally alert and raring to get work done (this was my preference—find your favourite time slot of the day and tweak your schedule around it). I used this time for everything from writing notes and preparing for the next day (if the school term was on) to solving questions on paper.

> **TIP**
> Use this time predominantly for writing.

Note: These aren't the time brackets in which I studied. The time periods are just divisions of the day that worked for me, broadly. If I studied early in the morning, I didn't study late at night, and vice versa. Most people sleep for about six to eight hours a day, as should you. I always made sure that I was well rested and never compromised on my sleep. I would adjust my study patterns by pushing them forward or backward. If you study till midnight, you might wake up at 7 or 8 the next morning. If you study till later, you'll have to wake up later. If you want to wake up at 5 a.m., you might have to sleep at 10 p.m. or 11 p.m.

After a good night's sleep, you'll likely have more energy and a higher ability to concentrate the next day.

Tweak the above structure to create your own personalized schedule that caters to your strengths.

What you need to do

Everyone thinks they know what the best time to study is, but the reality is that every person is different. Most people do not proactively test what works for them. They study when they 'feel like', but that's not necessarily their most effective time. So to know confidently what truly works for you, it's important to try something consistently for an extended length of time, then try something else, and afterwards compare the results. You should make an informed decision in choosing which times to test in the first place. There are some people who get more out of studying at night, while there are others who find the best time to study is the morning or the afternoon.

But finding the best time to study needs some self-experimentation. To arrive at the most optimal time for you, you need to start by studying at any time that you feel works best. Try it for a week before you try another time bracket, and then compare how well you did at both times:

▶ Was there a period in which you felt sleepy, lethargic or found yourself dozing off?

▶ When were you subject to less distractions? This could include distractions arising from social media, friends, family, etc.

▶ Was there a period that was less noisy?

▶ Was there a period in which you felt more focused, energetic and keen to get some work done?

Keep track of the answers to questions such as these. Once you have tried out different times of the day to study and decided which one works best for you, your job is to learn all the tough subjects during that time, so as to accomplish more and get better results.

5 tips for night-time studying

If you believe that you study more effectively at night, follow these tips to get the most out of your study time:

1. Establish a routine

If you decide to study at night, don't do it irregularly. Instead, make sure you establish a study routine. This will ensure that your body gets used to the new patterns and environment, and you can maximize your output. If you keep alternating and studying during the day for some time and then decide to change it and study at night, your body will go crazy! Pick one time period and stick to it.

2. Rest

If you study at night, by no means should that translate to you sleeping less. A well-rested mind is crucial for a successful study session, so make sure you don't neglect your sleep by taking a few hours to nap during the day. Also make sure you keep track of your break times, so you can focus on finishing what you have planned for the day.

3. Lighting

It can happen to us all—you start studying in the evening and the next thing you know, it's night-time and you're studying in the dark! Don't let this become a common occurrence. Make sure to study in a properly lit room, as it will improve your concentration. A dimly lit environment will start making you feel drowsy. It will also strain your eyes and, before you know it, your head and eyes will be on fire. Worse, your concentration level will be far lower, as you'll find yourself struggling against sleepiness instead of figuring out why 2+2 equals 4 and not 5. And that means that your study session won't be as effective as you want it to be, and you'll end up wasting precious time redoing it all the next day.

4. Time management
It's easy to lose track of time when studying at night. This makes it even more important to create a study timetable outlining when you will take breaks. As I've already said, I recommend taking a five- to ten-minute break every twenty to forty minutes when studying.

5. Music
Some people encourage listening to music while studying. It is believed that music helps reduce the boredom or loneliness that can creep in when studying alone at night. Light, repetitive music—preferably instrumental, which isn't very distracting—playing softly in the background has been found to be especially effective when people are doing mathematical problems. I, however, stayed away from listening to music while studying, because as a musician, I found that it diverted my concentration from my studies to the music.

21

Where to Study

Another question that I'm asked surprisingly often is whether the place I studied in had an impact on my quality of preparation. To be honest, I hadn't thought about this at the time and wouldn't even have included this if I hadn't been made to think about it.

I feel there aren't any hard and fast rules about where you should study—of course, it goes without saying that you aren't going to get much work done if you're sitting in the middle of a dance club surrounded by a million people screaming their lungs out. Choosing a place where you can study without distractions is an obvious suggestion that I don't need to give you.

But yes, try to put your phone away while you're

studying. Use your breaks for checking Facebook, WhatsApp, YouTube, etc. (Back in 2008, there weren't any smartphones, so this didn't really apply to us. In fact, I didn't even have a mobile phone at the time—I got my first when I joined college.) One way I used to unwind at the end of the day was by watching an episode of my favourite TV show (I'm most certainly a pop culture nerd, and a proud one at that!). That was my guilty pleasure every day after I had achieved my objectives. But I would never succumb to the temptation of opening my laptop during study time. That was a rule I strictly adhered to, and so should you. Have a guilty pleasure, but don't let it impinge on your study time. Keep it as a reward at the end of the day. It'll give you something to look forward to when you're mentally exhausted. If you feel that you can't trust yourself with a laptop, hand it over to a parent or a sibling and instruct them to give it to you only for a certain period of time every day.

(Word of caution: If you give it to your best friends or sibling, please make sure you've logged out of your Facebook account, as I learnt the hard way, when my friends decided to have some fun at my expense by posting embarrassing status updates from my account. Lesson learnt—never trust your best friends with your social media account. And most certainly never underestimate their love for juvenile pranks.)

However, one interesting thing that emerged from

my discussions about the best place to study in was that a lot of people are very conservative about their location. Most people want reassurance that the study table is indeed the best place to get the maximum work done—a cold, Spartan environment devoid of anything fun in the near vicinity. And to a large extent, that isn't far from the truth.

But I've found that I was often most efficient when I was reading on my bed. I simply enjoy the process of reading more when I'm comfortable—it's just a personal preference. Of course, I also had to take care to not get too comfortable and fall asleep. But as opposed to reading, when I was doing anything that involved writing, I preferred studying at a table. A personal tic: I always studied under a yellow lamp. I felt I studied better under warm, yellowy conditions. Obviously, I know that the lamp could have been fluorescent green, for all I cared; it was just a psychological tic that helped me enjoy the process of studying more, and hence study better. Therefore, I made sure that I studied under conditions that I felt most comfortable in.

The point I'm trying to make is that there are no hard and fast rules here. Choose a place that's quiet, non-distracting and comfortable, and you should be fine! Just make sure that you leverage all the tools at your disposal to make the act of studying as enjoyable as possible. It's the small things that start to add up over time.

Appendix: Why you shouldn't multitask

Multitasking makes you less productive and more distracted, and hence reduces your output.

Students who study effectively focus on one thing at a time. So don't try to study while also replying to text messages, watching TV and checking your Twitter feed. Here are some suggestions to improve your concentration:

- Turn off notifications on your phone.
- Put your phone away, or put it on airplane mode.
- Log out of all instant-messaging programmes.
- Turn off the Internet access on your computer.
- Use an app like Freedom, which is designed to keep you away from the Internet for a certain period of time.
- Close all Internet browser windows that aren't related to the assignment you're working on.
- Clear the clutter from your study area.

Time Spent 'Studying'

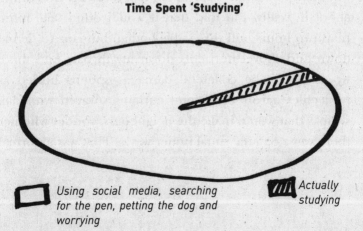

Using social media, searching for the pen, petting the dog and worrying

Actually studying

22

To Eat Or Not to Eat...

I've always been a huge proponent of a good diet. Let's just say I enjoy my food a certain way, much to the dismay of the people who are forced to eat my fairly insipid meals with me. But it wasn't always the case.

Growing up, I was a very picky eater. Family food time was more like family *feud* time. I hated eating. Everything about it, really. I'm told that it would often take more than two hours and three able-bodied humans to tie me down and shovel nutrients down my throat. And there would always be collateral damage—spoons hurled as projectiles across the room, curtains sprayed with dal, shrieks that would make the neighbours wonder whether there was a Satanic ritual under way... That was a normal day during lunch at the Sood family house, thanks to me.

My go-to excuse was to blame mum's cooking. Obviously. I would complain that her chapatis were bulletproof—I would hide them under the sofa cushions when she wasn't looking, and one day she found them when cleaning; let's just say she wasn't amused—and her chicken hard as rock.

I'm not entirely sure why my parents didn't just let me starve. But they did the next best thing—they packed me up and shipped me off to boarding school, and everything changed. That's when I found out what bulletproof chapatis really were and how chicken pieces could get so hard that they could pass for granite slabs. And midway through starvation, I suddenly began to appreciate food. My appreciation for food may also have had something to do with my introduction to the world of chicken nuggets, with the opening of this magical store called McDonald's in Dehradun, our small but not-so-sleepy town.

Eventually, I began to love food. And as I grew up, I began to get very interested in fitness and tennis. The interesting thing about the world of sports is that your diet will often be just as important, if not more, as the work that you put into hitting the weights or practising serves on the tennis court. You can spend hours in the gym, but if you don't follow it up with the right diet, all that effort will come to naught.

It's exactly the same for our brain. But what on earth is brain food?

Your brain uses 20 per cent of all glucose, 35 per cent of all vitamins and minerals, 40 per cent of all water and a staggering 50 per cent of all fats in your body, according to the website DevelopingHumanBrain. Foods that are best for nourishing our brains are those that have high amounts of nutrients, fats, water and just a little carb (or glucose). If you aren't getting the right nutrition from your food, your brain isn't getting what it needs to think and process information.

The bad news is that there isn't one particular food that fits this bill. You need a combination of them.

The good news is that they're all yum. Well, at least some of them are.

Here are some brain foods that you should incorporate into your diet, courtesy of research done by DevelopingHumanBrain:

1. Go nuts!

There are many kinds of nuts out there—and they're all good for you. They're nutritious and easy to eat. You can also easily toss them into other foods or carry them around with you as a snack.

How can nuts improve your brain health, you ask? Here's how:

Walnuts

▶ Help process information faster
▶ Help retain information
▶ Improve mood
▶ Help develop neurotransmitters in the brain

Almonds

▶ Improve memory
▶ Increase attention
▶ Enhance problem-solving skills

Cashews

▶ Improve memory

2. An apple a day keeps the doctor away

You know this old saying, don't you? It's true, at least as far as the memory doctor is concerned. Apples contain high levels of acetylcholine that help improve cognitive function. Apples also reduce stress. A research study showed that students who ate an apple at lunch showed as much as a 7-point increase in test scores during afternoon exams.

3. Definitely fishy

Fish such as salmon are high in healthy omega-3 fatty acids. These fats are important for making new neural pathways, which, in turn,

- ▶ Boost learning capacity
- ▶ Improve memory
- ▶ Improve cognitive functions

If you're not fond of fish, here are other foods rich in omega-3 fatty acids:

- Flaxseed
- Pumpkin seeds
- Walnuts

4. Dark is healthy

Dark chocolate is not only delicious, but also healthy. Who would have thought? Dark chocolate contains nutrients that help increase blood flow, improve cardiac functions and increase blood circulation to the brain. This in turn:

- ▶ Reduces stress
- ▶ Improves problem-solving skills
- ▶ Improves memory
- ▶ Increases focus

So go ahead and snack on dark chocolates. Just make sure you avoid chocolates with too much sugar.

5. Popeye, and mum, were right

You're probably groaning as you read this, but it turns out that mum (who's probably rubbing her hands in glee right now) was right all along. Green vegetables are a vital source of vitamins in the run-up to the exams. Most dark greens like spinach, kale and broccoli are packed with vitamin K, which helps build pathways in the brain. They are also a great source of vitamins B6 and B12, which help improve memory and focus. Green vegetables might not be your favourite food in the world, but at least you won't be dozing off any time soon.

6. ...So was Joe Black

Most people will tell you that peanut butter is unhealthy, but that couldn't be farther from the truth. Peanut butter is an excellent snack that contains lots of healthy calories that come from fats and proteins. Additionally, it's versatile. You can add it to pretty much anything, and it'll all taste great. For example, you could spread it on toast with honey—an absolutely delicious and healthy combination. As long as you don't burn the toast and set the kitchen on fire, even the least skilled chef can make a great peanut butter sandwich with just a slice of bread and a jar of the stuff. Alternatively, you could just eat it straight from the jar with a spoon (like Brad Pitt did in *Meet Joe Black*)! Try to find one without added sugar, to get all the benefits of the peanut butter without the unhealthy calories that sugar adds. If nothing else, throw some peanuts in your mum's blender, with some salt and honey to taste, and blend—there's nothing better than home-made peanut butter!

7. Coffee versus green tea

Caffeine is known to provide a quick jolt of energy that can help you focus on the task at hand and prevent your mind from wandering. For this very reason, it is often consumed by fitness enthusiasts before hitting the gym to improve the productivity of their workouts. In a similar vein, caffeine can provide a useful boost if consumed just prior to an exam. It will give you a surge of energy and help you focus your thoughts for a short period of time.

Having said that, it should be consumed in moderation. Consume too much, and all of a sudden you'll find yourself unable to focus properly during an exam—the exact opposite effect caffeine has in the short term. For the record, I've never felt the need to take caffeine—there are far healthier foods out there. Traditional sources of caffeine include coffee and energy drinks. I'd stay away from the latter at all costs, as they invariably contain high amounts of sugar and chemicals that can give you the 'sugar high and crash', which will drain your energy during an exam.

Avoid becoming dependent on coffee. I've met many people who've gotten so addicted to coffee that they can't function effectively without drinking copious amounts every day. They find themselves fatigued and unable to concentrate without their daily caffeine fix. Addiction is never a good thing, at least not to something like this. There's nothing wrong with a cup of coffee now and then, but never get to a point where you can't concentrate without coffee.

The alternative that I would recommend is green tea, as it provides antioxidants and boosts your concentration. It contains no sugar, is natural and one of the healthiest drinks out there.

8. Say yes to fresh fruit

If you need extra energy, consume fruits such as bananas, apples and oranges. They are delicious, healthy and natural. Not to mention that your mum will love you for it.

9. Answer the choline call

A while back, researchers from Boston University conducted a study on 1,400 adults over ten years. Their research indicated that participants who had diets high in choline performed better on memory tests. Choline converts into acetylcholine in our bodies and is essential for the creation of new memories.

Here's a list of foods that contain high amounts of choline:
- Chicken
- Eggs (the yolk contains 90 per cent of the choline in the egg)

- Lentils
- Sunflower seeds
- Pumpkin seeds
- Almonds
- Cabbage
- Cauliflower
- Broccoli

When studying, how often have we found ourselves reaching for that box of chocolates or bag of chips? For some reason, studying and gorging on food have always gone together. There's nothing more fun than munching on something while plodding through coursework. The only problem is that the foods we typically consume are those that prevent us from attaining the best possible results that we're capable of.

By eating some of the foods listed in this chapter instead, you will provide your body with healthy nutrients that will best fuel your preparation. Having said that, none of the foods mentioned above are enough on their own—they just won't cut it. For a healthy diet, it is important to strike a balance. That's why your goal should be to combine different foods at different times to get the best possible amount of nutrients.

One of the best combinations of healthy snacks is a mix of fresh fruit and nuts. For example, a simple combination of apple and peanuts will give you healthy fats and just a little bit of sugar for energy. Apples are also packed with fast-acting antioxidants that help reduce any stress you might be feeling because of your studies.

Which now brings us to frequency and proportions. The age-old question—three big meals or six small ones? Typically, the older generation will swear by the standard three big meals rule, and while many newer researchers and dieticians swear by the habit of eating many small meals, both have their advantages—science hasn't come to any definitive conclusion yet.

From my experience, I've found that eating smaller meals and snacking frequently was good for studying. Eating big meals can trigger your body into releasing hormones that cause drowsiness. How often have you found yourself feeling sleepy after a big lunch and dosing off while reading? If you only eat three meals, you will also feel hungry for long stretches of time, which will trigger the release of hormones that will take your attention away from studying.

I found it best to eat the foods mentioned above in small portions many times during the day. That helped keep my brain engaged, my stomach quiet, my nutrition and energy levels up, and my distractions low.

Brain foods for exam day

Make sure you have a decent meal (breakfast or lunch) before leaving for your exam hall. Eat food that is too heavy, and you'll feel sleepy during the exam. Eat food that is too liquidy, and you'll risk feeling nauseous. Eat food that is too light, and you'll be sacrificing energy that you'll need for the three-hour exam ahead of you.

For example, an optimum breakfast would be some oats or porridge and a two- to three-egg omelette with spinach and mushrooms cooked in a touch of olive oil, followed by a fruit such as an apple. You could even throw in a handful of nuts—almonds would be perfect.

Assuming that you haven't added sugar to the oats or porridge (and hopefully not to the omelette), your breakfast will contain minimal sugar and be high in the nutrients that matter. The oats provide the complex carbohydrates, the eggs provide the proteins, the olive oil and nuts provide the healthy fats, and the fruit provides the fibre and natural sugars. Such a breakfast will break down slowly in your body, ensuring that the energy is released slowly over time and that you feel full for longer. As an added bonus, at the very least, you can be certain that you won't be the person whose stomach decides that it's time to erupt, and starts to grumble in a dead-silent exam hall, disrupting everyone's concentration within a five-mile radius!

On the other hand, what does a bad breakfast look like?

A bad breakfast would be a pastry, sugary coffee or cereal. These foods are low in the necessary nutrition and high in sugar, which will give you a sugar crash during your exam.

To conclude, the food that we eat will have a huge impact not just on our board preparations, but also on our health—quite possibly something that is far more important than any exam will ever be. What we eat impacts the way our body and brain behave. On a more superficial level, what we eat impacts the way we look, and the way we look impacts the way we perceive ourselves and, hence, the way we feel. And the way we feel affects our confidence—important in its own right, because that has a ripple effect on a lot of other things, our board examinations included. So, put that bag of chips aside and pick up that box of almonds that you've been hiding from. As a bonus, mum will be thrilled.

23

The Power of Preparation

Take a minute to introspect and answer the following questions.

Do you come unprepared to class?

Have you slept through class thinking to yourself that this is all a waste of time?

Do you pay less attention to your schoolteacher, because you think you'll be studying the same thing in tuitions?

Be honest.

Now do this calculation:

▸ Average school duration = 6 hours a day
▸ Number of schooldays per week = 5 (in some cases 6)

▸ Number of weeks of school in an academic year (assuming three months of vacation) = 39

Therefore, the total number of hours spent in school during an academic year = 6 * 5 * 39 = 1,170 hours

You will spend 1,170 hours of your 12th grade in school. That's the equivalent of 48 days: more than one and a half months.

If you answered 'yes' to any of the questions at the start of this chapter, as I did a few years back, I have news for you. You're wasting one and a half months of preparation time, and that could have a huge impact on your final results.

Think of it this way—besides perhaps sleeping in class, you can't really do anything else during those 1,170 hours, can you? You can't play your favourite sport, you can't go meet your best friend, you can't watch a movie—you're stuck in class for those 1,170 hours. So why not put those hours to good use, and then use some of that extra time you've bought yourself to extend your break once you're back home? That's one way of looking at it.

So how do we take these 1,170 hours and make the most of our time in school?

Reinforce your concepts

The good news is we've already done all the hard work, and there's nothing that we really need to go out of our way to do to maximize our school time. The answer lies in the notes we've been making. Because we've started early, we've already made notes for each upcoming class. And because of the way that we've gone about it, our notes will cover everything that our teacher will in the lecture, and then some.

So when it's time for class, use the lecture as a way to revise (and maybe improve) the notes you've already made. I've discussed the power of reinforcement before. Use the lectures to reinforce your concepts. This is how you're going to cement them in your head.

Read your topic notes the night before, come to class prepared and notice that you're ahead of your classmates

If you can, try to skim through your notes the night before. By doing so, you'll be well versed with the concepts your classmates are only just being introduced to. You'll be able to engage with the schoolteacher in classroom discussions at a higher level than the rest of your class. Being ahead of your class and seeing it for yourself will increase your confidence and bolster your conviction in the endeavour we've embarked upon.

And I've talked about the importance of confidence numerous times so far.

Develop that 'feel good' sensation

When you see yourself being ahead of the rest of the class, you'll start to feel better about your preparation. Seeing positive results will give you the impetus to work harder, because you'll enjoy the feeling of being the best. It's an addictive feeling that I'll cover later in this book.

Appendix: Try being a frontbencher

This may not be the coolest advice you were hoping to receive, but if you get to choose where you sit during class, grab a seat at the front, even if only for this year. Sure, it might attract some 'nerd' labels that might mildly damage your 'street-cred', but it'll be worth it.

Studies have shown that students who prefer to sit at the front tend to get higher scores in exams (Rennels & Chaudhari, 1988). Depending on where students sit, their average scores are as follows (Giles, 1982):

- Front rows: 80 per cent
- Middle rows: 71.6 per cent
- Back rows: 68.1 per cent

Now, in the above case, the seats were assigned by a teacher. So it's not *just* a case of more motivated students choosing to sit at the front getting more marks. A seat in one of the front rows means you'll be able to see the board better and hear the teacher more clearly, and your concentration, too, will improve. Plus, there's a bonus here—you can't hide behind your best friend and doze off, and are forced to engage with the teacher.

When your friends see you sitting in the first row.

24

Tuitions

The Indian school education system today has become synonymous with evening coaching classes—or tuitions, as we like to call them. A question I'm asked a lot by parents is: Should I send my kid for coaching? Today, it's almost a given that to get the highest grades, you have to take extra help in the evenings.

It's a cycle that is promulgated by a couple of factors. The first is the parents' general belief that without tuition, their kid won't have that *edge* against every other kid on the planet going for extra lessons. Second is the view of the kids, which is that because they anyway have to go for tuition in the evenings, they don't really need to pay attention in class. For this reason, all of a sudden, tuitions become far more important than they need to be. You can sleep through school and catch up on what you missed in tuition later. Some teachers recognize the potential tuition classes have for earning a steady supplementary income and start condoning the students' attitude. And the cycle continues.

Tuition, then, becomes the main avenue for education, instead of the supplementary source it was originally intended to be. That's where I believe we're getting it wrong. I don't have anything against taking tuitions—in fact, I would encourage it when required. But there are the two key words—*when required*.

As for me, I took tuition. All credit goes to my mum and dad, who did the research to find the best tutors within their budget and then spent all their free time picking up and dropping me to various extra classes. Because I studied in a boarding school, I could only take tuition over the summer and winter breaks—three months in the year. But I realized that the tuitions had a high cost for my parents—not only when it came to their finances but also when it came to their time and energy. I appreciated that and made sure that I tried my best to make the most of these classes.

So far, we're assuming that you've inculcated (or have committed to inculcate) the habits that we've gone over to maximize your results. This includes taking the right notes, paying attention in school, etc. If you're with us so far, let's continue.

Alright. So, tuition. Like I have said before, don't just do something because everyone else is doing it. If you're part of the herd, you'll never lead the way. Don't just take evening classes because everyone else is taking them. Once you feel that you're paying attention in class, making your notes and doing everything that you possibly can to maximize your results (if you follow the book, you will be), then think about whether taking extra evening lessons will benefit you.

Tuitions are a supplement

Remember to treat tuitions as the supplementary source of education and not the primary one. The primary driver should be you—your notes, your effort, your motivation. Tuitions are just here to give you a boost. All those around you, who treat tuitions as the be all and end all of their 12th-grade preparations, will never make it to where you're headed.

That said, if you are taking tuition classes, here's how you can make the most of them.

1. The right tutor
When choosing which tuition to attend, I can't stress enough the importance of a good teacher. The right one can make all the difference. I was lucky that my

parents went out of their way to find the best tutors within their budget. They asked around—friends, other parents, teachers, even kids a year older—to find out who the more respected tutors in town were. Work with your parents to do the same. Do not succumb to the temptation of going to a tutor because all your friends are going there. For this one year (at the very least), you have to chart and tread your own path.

One thing most of my tutors had in common was they didn't waste any time. They made us write, write, write, and then write some more. They gave us notes and they made us write out answers to questions. Make sure you find a tutor who is a hard taskmaster and will push you that extra mile.

2. The duration

The problem with year-long coaching is that it drags on much longer than it needs to. The students and the teachers both know that they have a full year ahead of them, and they tend to take it easy. That's the last thing you want to do in your board year. I only attended coaching three months in my 12th grade, and in retrospect, that worked out perfectly. The coaching was intense; the tutor and the students couldn't afford to waste any time, and we made sure we didn't. As it turns out, three months is the perfect duration to comfortably finish the full year's syllabus.

3. Finances

Another advantage of a shorter, more intense tuition period is that you can now spend higher per class, assuming your parents have a fixed budget. This is a crucial point most parents don't factor in. Often, some of the best tutors in town are the most expensive (not a rule, but this is a fair assumption to make these days. More people go to them because they are good tutors. As demand goes up, so does their asking price). It's possible that you might not be able to afford studying with them all the year round (not that you'll need to anyway). Taking coaching for a shorter, say three-month, period allows you the option of spending more per class. Alternatively, you now also have the option of studying in a smaller group size, as these tend to be more expensive than larger batch tuitions. Which brings us to...

4. The study-group size

This is purely personal preference, but the ideal group size should lie somewhere between one and six students. The smaller the group, the more personal attention you will get. In smaller groups (or in one-on-one coaching), you'll be able to clarify each doubt that you have (and you should have a bagful of doubts). The lessons will be tailored to your needs and will, therefore, benefit you more.

However, some people enjoy reviewing their materials with a group of friends or classmates. Such groups work best when they are kept small (four or five others), with people of similar academic aptitude. The advantage of such study groups is that they:

▸ Facilitate debate and an exchange of ideas. In this case, try to make sure that you're surrounded by a bunch of students who are smart and eager to learn. Such a peer group will push you to become better.

▸ Help you arrive at new perspectives. If you study on your own, you'll always view your subject from the same lens—yours. Getting a new perspective on a subject can help you learn more thoroughly. Study groups are the perfect places to challenge yourself. You will be surrounded by different viewpoints on topics. This will force you to think more about your position, and will, therefore, develop your critical-thinking skills while helping you study.

▸ Allow you to improve your study method. Over time, you will have developed your own study method. While yours may work seamlessly, you can find means to improve it. By joining a study group, you'll observe a variety of study methods and can then develop your own routine by integrating the best methods with your own.

▶ Break the monotony. Studying on your own can become monotonous over extended periods of time. Because of the social aspect of a study group, you will always have someone to discuss the topic with when you start struggling or find the topic tedious. In addition, the auditory factor of study groups can help utilize an extra sensory means to retain knowledge.

▶ Fill in learning gaps. By comparing notes with other students, you can evaluate your accuracy, fix any errors and get ideas for better note-taking.

In such groups, effective ways to imbibe knowledge are:

▶ Working through chapters together.

▶ Quizzing one another as you go through chapters.

▶ Comparing class notes and reviewing material to ensure that you haven't missed any critical point.

As you can see, study groups can be helpful for many students, but not all. So it is worth spending some time introspecting about what has worked best for you in the past, before you decide on the kind of environment you want to study in.

25

How to Tackle a Question Paper

It's crucial to know how to answer a question paper properly. Take the example of my brother Rishi, who, despite being one of the smartest people I know, struggled to answer question papers effectively for the longest time. He could quote Shakespeare at the drop of a hat, but put an exam paper in front of him and he wouldn't be able to write an answer to save his life.

Why was it so?

There were a couple of reasons. He wasn't very good at preparing for an exam. He struggled with time management and was unable to allocate resources effectively. He also thought that taking notes was below him.

But, with my help, he worked on slowly improving on all these parameters, using the methods I've outlined so far. Eventually, he also got into St Stephen's College, where he studied Economics, and is currently studying at the Indian Institute of Management, Bangalore (IIMB). Even though taking exams didn't come naturally to him, he managed to attend two of the best institutions in the world. (Unbeknownst to the both of us at the time, he happened to be my first test subject!)

But the one thing he struggled with the most was dealing with the question paper. It wasn't just him—I have seen the same thing happen to my girlfriend in college. She was one of the most resourceful people I knew—she was clever, focused and hard-working—but, like my brother, she didn't know what to do with a question paper.

So here's how to deal with one:

1. Improve your confidence

The first thing to do is to improve your preparation. That is the foundation—without knowing the syllabus like the back of your hand, there's no point even reading this chapter. Luckily for us, we've already covered that in the previous chapters. You have to have confidence in yourself, and that'll only develop once you have confidence in your preparation.

By this point, you should be able to walk into the

exam hall right this instant and say with conviction, 'No matter what the exam throws at me, my preparation will allow me to answer it effectively.' If you don't have that confidence yet, you're not ready. You'll always be nervous and keep second-guessing yourself in the exam hall, and your answers will suffer.

2. Keep the answer the right length

Once you're confident that your preparation is adequate, it's up to you to decide how you want to present the information in your head in the form of an answer. Too long an answer, and you risk losing the interviewer's attention. Too short, and you risk leaving out essential information. One of my teachers at The Doon School once said, '*The perfect answer is like a miniskirt—long enough to cover the essentials but short enough to remain interesting.*' I don't think I could ever put it more succinctly or, well, poetically than that.

I can't make a blanket statement about the correct length of an answer here—that's something you'll be able to arrive at by following the methods outlined in the book. I hope you understand that there are far too many variables that make it impossible for me to do so, except on a case-by-case, subject-by-subject and topic-by-topic basis—which I'd be happy to do for you if you reach out to me.

3. Leave time for revision

You must get into the habit of leaving at least ten minutes for revision after you've finished writing your paper. I can't stress how important this is. No matter how well we think our paper has gone, we all make mistakes. A quick ten-minute revision is almost always more than sufficient to spot and rectify those errors. There's no worse feeling than the helplessness and frustration you go through once you realize that you've made a silly mistake you could easily have fixed, but only after you've stepped out of the exam hall. You can count on the revision to improve your grade by at least two to five marks.

4. Read instructions carefully

On most occasions, if not all, you'll have the chance to know the exam pattern prior to the exam date. However, you never know when the exam decides to throw a curveball. It happens more often than you realize. So read the instructions carefully to make sure that you don't make an easily avoidable mistake.

5. Do not answer an extra question

As a follow-up to the previous point, do not answer a question that you are not supposed to. You'll end up wasting valuable time and get nothing for it. In fact, you'll only sacrifice your own marks, because you'll have that much less time to finish the rest of your paper. Read the question prompts very, very carefully before you start writing your answers.

6. Choose the right question

This is a skill you'll develop only after you've answered numerous questions with paper and pen over the course of your preparation. There are often questions for which the answers seem easy in your head, but when you get down to writing them out, seem far more difficult to express. And by the time you realize this in the exam hall, it's too late to backtrack, and you find yourself getting more and more nervous with each minute. In such a scenario, you won't just end up doing a poor job answering the question, you'll also risk answering the rest of your paper poorly because you're panicking.

7. Submit a presentable paper

Give your examiner a paper to read that won't give him or her a squint, will you please? Otherwise be a gem and attach a pair of reading glasses with your answer sheet for his benefit. Or you could just try to be neat. You could take it a step further and write with two different-coloured pens for the ease of legibility.

It isn't just about legibility. It's important that you frame your answer in a way that the most important parts catch the examiner's eye. And like I've said before, these are the parts that will get you the marks. If they're buried somewhere deep in a long-winded answer, chances are that the examiner might miss them and give you a poor grade. We've talked about this in the chapter on how to answer a question.

A lot of people get away with this, but give it some thought. A good fraction of the papers the examiner will go through will be poorly presented. Why, then, would you give up a chance to stand out from rest of the hundreds with a tweak that will cost you no extra effort? It can only help. While you may not receive any explicit tangible benefit from presenting a neat, legible paper, you can rest assured that doing so will please your examiner. And a happy examiner is always better than an indifferent one.

What if you're running short on time?

For whatever reason, there's always a chance that we might find ourselves in the unenviable position of losing the race against the clock. What do we do in such a scenario?

If such a scenario were indeed to arise, the odds are that it will happen towards the tail end of the exam, when you just have your last answer to go. In such a scenario, prioritize.

If you're running out of time:

▸ **Forget the niceties.**
   Forget about the perfect introduction that you
   were planning, or the calculations that you were

going to show. It's time for you to consolidate all of that into as small a step as you can manage.

▶ **Play the money card first.**

Your job now is to put across the most important topics/ideas/arguments/calculations right at the beginning.

▶ **Use bullet points and abbreviated sentences, if required.**

Examiners sometimes prefer bullet points, which are easier to read than lengthy sentences. There's a good chance that, for this reason, bullet points can work in your favour now.

▶ **Work your way down the ladder of importance.**

The most important parts of your answer should be right on top. Chances are that if you mention the most important few points at the beginning, the examiner will assume that you know your answer and will give you the full score without bothering to read the less important points later.

▶ **Don't leave it hangin…**

Even if you haven't been able to put in all the points that you wanted to in your answer, spend that last minute writing a conclusion to wrap it up. Do not waste that last minute trying to add another point. The examiner is far more likely to notice that the answer is incomplete if there's no proper ending, and may decide to penalize you for it, as opposed to noticing that a less important point is missing. Remember, you've already written the most important parts of the answer at the beginning. Those should be enough to get you the marks. You don't want to show the examiner that you ran out of time. He will dock a mark if he notices that.

You don't want to leave your last sentence like this, do y...'

Alternatively, if you find yourself with more than one question to solve and only enough time to answer one, here are my tips:

▶ **Prioritize**
Choose the question that is easier to answer and tackle that first. This might be a question that you know the answer to perfectly, or it might be an objective question, as opposed to a subjective one, or it might be a question that involves calculations, as opposed to descriptions. Choose the one that will fetch you the maximum marks in the minimum possible time.
Alternatively, if the calculation is too long to complete in time **(remember that it's harder to do math when you're under pressure)**, it might be smarter to go for a descriptive answer. Leaving a descriptive answer incomplete can still fetch

you marks, perhaps more so than an incomplete calculation or definition.

▶ **Don't have time to answer both? Answer both!** This might seem counter-intuitive, but using the points from the above section (answering a single question when running short on time), try to answer both the questions. I'll explain why.

Let's say that both questions, which are for 10 marks each, require descriptive answers. Were you to take all the time to write the perfect answer for one, maybe you'll get a 10, maybe you'll get an 8. Since you've left out the other question, you'll definitely get a 0 there. Your total? $8/10 + 0/10 = 8/20$.

On the other hand, assume that you incorporate inputs from the above section and submit two abbreviated answers. Because of the reasons mentioned above, chances are that you'll score 6 or 8 on both questions. It's also possible (even likely) that, if you've followed my advice, you might actually get the same score as you might have got had you answered the question perfectly. In this case, you might get an $8/10$ on both answers. Add up the first case? $6/10 + 6/10 = 12/20$. And the second? $8/10 + 8/10 = 16/20$. In both cases, you're better off than if you'd only answered one question perfectly.

The reason for this is that, because we've prepared so well, chances are that, in our quest to provide the perfect answer, we have provided the examiner with more than is required. Say, instead of providing one example, we've provided two; we've added some figures and dates; we've provided an illustration; we've shown extra steps of calculation, just to be safe. But chances are that we'll still get the perfect score, even if we don't provide some of these details.

Q7. Find c

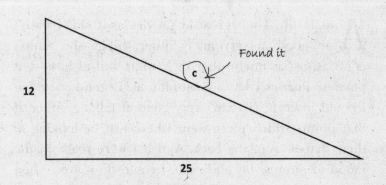

How 'not to' tackle a question paper.

26

Identifying Exam Patterns

Apparently, I was great at puzzles as a kid. I wasn't too good at very many other things—I couldn't crawl as fast as my brother or bawl as well as him—but puzzles? Puzzles I was a champion at. Legend goes that I could indicate (I wasn't very good at talking either at that point) which piece went where just by looking at their shapes from the back. And if I were really in the mood to impress my audience, I could do it even when the pieces of multiple puzzle games had been mixed together, potpourri-style. I would just point at the pieces and then point at whichever part of whichever puzzle they belonged to. All while sitting on my blue porta-potty, I'm told.

These 'skills' came to my rescue several years later, when I decided to try to understand exam papers. Now, exam papers can be fickle creatures. Board examinations usually give you a choice. These choices come in different forms—question types and topics. Some questions may have subjective answers, others may ask questions from the toughest topic in the book. The toughest choices (and thereby the toughest papers) force you to choose between a high-risk-high-reward question (a short, objective answer to a tough question) and a low-risk-low-reward question (a long, subjective answer to an easy question).

The decision you make might be the difference between a good and a great score. Take one route, and you might get that perfect grade; take the other and you might not. Your fate is literally in your hands—which is what makes the choice so important.

Apart from officially stated patterns, I would advise against trying to predict what your paper might look like, especially given how thorough our preparation will have been so far. The simple fact is that we won't need to. Having said that, it's a good idea to study past papers for patterns (as opposed to predictions).

Why are we identifying patterns?

Patterns can help us decide what kind of questions we'd prefer answering, were the choice presented to us. Think of it like deciding what to buy at a department store before even entering it. You know the store probably has the candy and the chocolate you love. You don't want to be the one holding up the line because you couldn't for the life of you choose between Snickers and Twix (always Twix), do you? The choice becomes even more confusing when your eyes fall on the candy section—do you go for the candies or do you stick with the chocolates? Both are yum! The same analogy works for the exam paper. Think of candies as question types and chocolates as topics.

Decoding a pattern will help save time on the final day, because you'll know what kind of questions and topics you'd prefer answering, and you'll avoid wasting time trying to make up your mind. This will leave you with more time to tackle your answer the way you want to.

How do we decode an exam pattern?

1. **Start by reading the exam papers vertically.**
   To start with, glance through each exam paper in the Last Ten Years' Papers vertically, from top to bottom, as you would any normal paper. The idea here is to get a feel of the question types and the general layout of the paper.
2. **Then read the exam papers horizontally across the years.**
   To successfully decode a pattern, it's crucial to analyse the papers horizontally across the years.

For example, go section-wise across the years and see what kinds of questions are asked in each section.

Now you should be in a position to:

3. **Identify common topics in each section.**
   You should now be in a better position to tell what parts of the course are generally covered in the different sections and...

4. **Identify common question types in each section.**
   You should be in a position to identify the question types by now—long answers, short answers, numerical answers, definitions, etc.

5. **Notice the kind of choice the papers present.**
   Finally, you should be able to tell what kind of choices you're presented with in each section. Do you have to solve one out of two questions or do you get to choose one out of five? It's important to take note of these factors. A wider choice means that you'll have wiggle room to decide on your favourite question type or topic, and perhaps favour those during your preparation.

6. **Decide which of the question types you're most comfortable with.**
   By this stage in your preparation, you should know where you stand when it comes to different question types—some people prefer short, objective answers; some prefer to stay away from

mathematical questions and would rather attempt long, essay-type questions. Know what you're best at.

7. **Rank these topics in order of your comfort level.** It's important to know where your strengths and weaknesses lie, not only when it comes to the question type, but also when it comes to different topics. Play to your strengths and tackle the topics you're most comfortable with first.

Pro Tips

▶ Short, objective answers (especially the ones that contain calculations) have the biggest risk-reward ratio. That means if you get such a question right, you're sure to get a full score, but if you don't, you get less than an average score.

▶ There's more scope to get a great (but not perfect) score in longer answers.

▶ My advice would be to go for the short, objective questions if you're sure about them. They'll buy you more time, and you can be assured of a perfect score (if you've answered them correctly).

▶ However, if you're not sure about your answer, it's safer to go with the longer answers, where you can still get away with a less-than-perfect answer with a good-enough (or even perfect, although less likely) score. However, keep an eye on the time.

For the record, I went with the short, objective, numerical answers wherever I had the choice, because I was confident in my preparation and because it saved me time.

27

Simulating Exam Day

The last point on our checklist to cement our preparation and knock the ball out of the stadium is to try and simulate the final day.

Why do we do this?

We're going to be nervous on the day of the exam—and that's completely normal. In fact, there's nothing you can do that will eliminate those nerves completely. And being nervous is a good thing to an extent. It shows that you care about how well you do and how badly you want it. But being too nervous can play games with your mind and make things harder—you won't be able to think as clearly, you'll second-guess your calculations, your hand won't move as fast as it's used to, etc.

While we can't get rid of the nerves completely, we can try to minimize them by recreating the exam setting the best we can. As I've mentioned before, familiarity breeds comfort, which, in turn, helps settle our nerves on the final day. Take an official board-examination paper and try to solve it in the required time period. Make sure you write out your answers in full, as you would on the final day. Since you've already been timing yourself on individual questions (if you've followed the book), you should have no problems answering the entire question paper well within the time limit. But answering a single question is different from answering a three-hour paper in one go. The purpose of this exercise is to not only prepare you for the final day but also to improve stamina and concentration.

Keep the following things in mind:

▸ Strictly adhere to the time limit.
▸ Solve the paper during the same time of day that the paper is scheduled to take place. So if you know that the Mathematics paper is scheduled for 2 p.m. on the actual day of the exam, begin your mock Math paper at 2 p.m. sharp as well.
▸ Do not take breaks.
▸ Solve the paper at a desk in a quiet environment.
▸ Do not eat or drink anything while solving the paper.

▶ Write out each answer in full, as you would on the final day.

Make sure you do this for all subjects.

If you really want to challenge yourself, try the following (do this only once per subject and only if you have the time to spare):

▶ Reduce the time limit by half an hour. So if the paper duration is three hours, set your timer for 2.5 hours, and try to complete the entire paper in this attenuated time frame. It is important to note that by no means should you sacrifice the quality of your answer when you do this. The goal is to think more efficiently and write faster, not shorter.

▶ Solve the paper in a noisy environment that is full of distractions. The increased difficulty will force you to concentrate harder. Next time you're solving a paper in a quiet environment, you'll be surprised at how much easier you find it. This will also come in handy in case your examination hall turns out to be noisier than you expected. You won't be distracted, whether there's a marriage procession passing by or a NASA space shuttle landing outside.

▶ Solve the paper on an empty stomach. You will

be low on energy and will find it harder to concentrate. This will prepare you for the off chance that your stomach is unsettled on the actual day.

Another way to reduce the nerves on the final day is to picture yourself taking the exam in the actual exam hall. Try to visit the examination hall a few weeks before the boards begin and acquaint yourself with the atmosphere. Go home and envision yourself writing the exam in that environment. Picture the invigilators walking by. Picture everyone around you. Picture the clock on the wall. If done correctly, you should notice yourself getting nervous. If you do this a few times (once every day or so), you'll start to feel comfortable in that environment and you'll gradually notice that you're less nervous each time you do this exercise. Spend a minute doing this, not more.

28

Pre-boards

The pre-board exams are your last stop before the final stretch. It's important to treat the pre-boards the same way that you would your final board exams.

There are a few things to note when it comes to the pre-boards:

1. They are almost always designed to be far harder than the actual exam.
So don't get nervous if you find that your question paper is more difficult than you thought it would be. It's set so that it comes across that way—it's meant to be more difficult than anything you might have come across so far.

2. They are structured to allow you enough time to shore up any last-minute weaknesses they might have revealed in your preparation.

You'll have enough time between your pre-boards and your boards to focus on any topic you feel you struggled with while giving your pre-boards. There's absolutely no need to panic—it's normal. Panicking will clutter your mind and significantly hamper your preparation at a time when you need to be at the top of your game.

3. The marking in the pre-boards will almost always be far stricter than in the board exams.

Gave a perfect paper only to receive a low score? Don't worry. Most teachers are instructed to be brutal when it comes to marking the pre-board papers. I've seen numerous 'perfect' answers get a 7/10. The point here is to be able to differentiate between when your teacher has been strict and when your answer has, in fact, been lacking. There isn't anything worse than attributing your poor grade to strict marking, when it was really your answer that was to blame.

4. The main aim of the pre-boards is not only to prepare you for the final exam but also to motivate you to put in that last bit of extra effort and go all out.

The most important use of the pre-boards, in my opinion, isn't the preparation, but the motivation. Like I said before, it's all about how you finish. There's nothing more important than the last leg of any race. Use the pre-boards to push yourself to give it everything, and then some, for the last and final stretch. Use the results that you obtain in the pre-boards as motivation to fuel your final preparation. This last stretch can make the difference between a great board result and that *perfect* board result.

WHEN THEY SET
THE PRE-BOARD EXAM PAPER

... AND JUST A
DASH OF DIFFICULT

OOPS!

Beyond the scope of the syllabus

Just as an aside, I'm sometimes asked about the benefits of going beyond the scope of the syllabus. While an admirable endeavour in its own right, it's perhaps not the best use of time for our purposes. Our goal this year is to top the boards, and not to acquire 'knowledge'. The chances of finding yourself staring at a question that is out of the scope of the syllabus, scratching your head and wondering where on earth it came from, are slim, to begin with.

If, by some small chance, such a question does make its way into your board paper, you will be granted the marks. Everyone will. For that reason, going beyond the scope of the syllabus can prove to be a waste of time, effort and brainpower. The syllabus in question is vast enough, as it is. Spend your time on another revision, if need be. Or maybe just go watch a movie.

29

The Curse of the Last Exam

Think of this scenario:

You've finished all but one exam paper. You're confident that you've done extremely well in the papers that you've given so far. All that remains is one last paper that is a few days away. People are discussing their holiday plans. You're thinking about college and how much fun it'll be to finally get out of your school uniform. Some friends have already finished their last paper, and there's a party on the horizon—all the cool kids will be there. The general ambience is one of farewell and goodbyes.

All your friends are having fun; your last exam, though, is still a few days away. But you tell yourself it won't hurt to spend a few days relaxing. After all, you deserve a break for working so hard over the last twelve months and for having given such good papers. Surely, it won't hurt to attend that party. Even your parents won't mind...

And before you know it, there's only one day left till the final paper. Kicking yourself for having let the last few days slip by, you're aware that your preparation has been less than ideal for this final paper. But you tell yourself that you'll manage. You've fared alright so far, haven't you?

The day of the paper arrives. You can barely concentrate on the task at hand. Everyone around you is full of excitement—people are already saying their goodbyes, tears are being shed. You're surrounded by people who have become your best buddies over the past few years. You've fought with them, grown up with them, laughed with them and cried with them.

Who cares about this last exam? It is just an insignificant paper. You might never see these guys in your life again, you think to yourself...

What do you think is going to happen in this scenario? Do you think you're in the right space mentally to ace that final paper? Do you know that that last *insignificant* paper could account for one-fifth of your final percentage? That's 20 per cent of your final overall grade right there. A few days of fun could ruin your entire year's efforts—everything you have worked so hard for over the last twelve months. All those late nights and tuitions and notes, all for naught.

Not so insignificant now, is it?

I've seen this happen year after year. I've seen it happen to my seniors. I've seen it happen to my classmates. I've seen it happen to kids every year without fail. For such a silly reason, I've seen people's percentages fall by more than 10 per cent.

If it had happened to me, everything else remaining the same, instead of a 99 per cent, I would have had an 89 per cent, and would have struggled to get into any college, let alone the college of my dreams. I would never have got the dream consulting job that everyone wants. I would never have got the scholarships that I received. I would never have met my best friends and I would never have met the most amazing girl on the planet. I would never have had the opportunities that those marks allowed me to experience.

Are those few days of fun worth it?

Not at all.

Don't let it happen to you. The last exam curse is very, very real. And it's the silliest way to ruin an entire year of hard work that you've put in.

Back to the tennis analogies for a quick minute. Maybe you've heard of the tennis legend Andre Agassi? Before one of the most important matches of his career, his coach said something to this extent (paraphrased): '*All I want you to do is just go out there and win the first and last point. It's as simple as that. I don't care about anything else.*' In tennis, the winner is the last man standing. The person who wins the last point is the person who wins the match. There are so many players who have been one point away from the championship only to crumble under the pressure and watch as the match slips away. And they have remained has-beens.

Tennis, like life, can be cruel sometimes.

There's a similar analogy in the world of fitness. There are trainers who say that the most important exercise is the last one of the day. Because by the time the last exercise set comes around, you've already spent an hour working out at the gym. Your body is tired, your muscles are screaming in pain and all you want to do is go home and dunk yourself in a cold shower. And you think to yourself that it's okay if you skip that last exercise. And sure, it's perfectly okay—that last exercise itself isn't magically going to turn you into Arnold Schwarzenegger. There's nothing special about it.

But it's all about your attitude. Because if you give up before the final exercise today, tomorrow you'll give up before the second-last and then the third-last, and so on. Winners don't give up. Winners don't quit. Winners tough it out. And you want to be a winner—not just in your board examinations but in everything else you do in life. Start thinking like a winner. It'll hold you in good stead.

The solution is simple—all it requires is a few days of mental discipline to be able to say no to distractions.

You'll have enough time with your school friends after the last exam bell rings. So do not get distracted during this final stretch. Remember that it is just for a few days and that those few days could make all the difference in the world.

For, as they say, it isn't over till the fat lady sings, is it now?

30

There's Many a Slip Between the Cup and the Lip

The boards have arrived and it's what you've worked so hard for the whole of last year. It's important to know that there will always be things that are out of your control. There's nothing you can do about a noisy marriage procession on the road as you're taking your exam. There's nothing you can do if the fan in the hall isn't working during your exam. If things can go wrong, they will go wrong. Accept that things will go off script and don't allow them to bother you, because there is nothing you can do about them. You don't want them to distract you.

Control the things you can. Your preparation, for

example—that is something you can control. So nail it. Minimize any chance of anything lowering your end result. For example, nobody cares if you had a stomach ache on the day of your exam. You'll get superficial sympathy, sure, but at the end of the day, it's the result that matters. No college or company cares about whether you were stuck in a traffic jam or had jaundice, typhoid, malaria or an upset stomach the day of your exam. There's no place for that on your résumé. So don't allow it to happen. Eat sensibly. Leave for the exam early, etc, etc.

Along those lines, here are a few things to keep in mind as the exam date approaches:

The day before the exam:

▶ It's perfectly normal to be nervous.

▶ Have faith in your preparation. You've given it everything you could.

▶ Spend the day before going over any last-minute definitions you might want to stay on top of.

▶ If possible, try to take the day off. You've earned it. It'll help recharge your batteries one final time. Give your hand a rest.

▶ Take a stationery check. Buy anything you might need. Extra pens, pencils, rulers, erasers, geometry sets, etc.

▶ Most importantly, stick to safe, bland food—at

least for a week or so before the exams! Make sure you don't eat anything that can give you an upset stomach. Being unable to concentrate during an exam is, without doubt, one of the easiest ways to ruin all your hard work.

▶ Sleep early! The boards is not the time for late-night cramming. If you've followed this book, there should be nothing left that you'll need to stay up for in the first place. It's more important to wake up feeling fresh.

The day of the exam:

▶ It's important to be in the optimal state of mind to take the exam to the best of your abilities. Food and nutrition have a huge role to play, as far as this is concerned. The food we eat impacts our energy levels, the way our body responds, the way we feel and, most importantly, how our brain functions.

To paraphrase from Chapter 22, *To Eat Or Not To Eat...*, make sure you consume a sensible meal before leaving for the exam hall. This includes portion size, food composition and nutrition profile (covered in Chapter 22).

Ensure that your meal isn't too heavy, or you'll feel sleepy during the exam. Worse, you might have a stomach ache, which is one of the most frustrating things to happen in an exam. Try to stick to dry foods, as too many liquids in your digestive system can make you sick and induce vomiting. This feeling is compounded by your nervous system that's functioning on overdrive. Simultaneously, your adrenal glands are doing their best to keep your body in *fight or flight mode*. This means that your body wants to get rid of any deadweight liquids inside it that might '*slow it down*'. It also shuts down or minimizes any resources diverted towards non-essential body functions, such as digestion, to maximize blood flow for more important ones. You have evolution to thank for this. This is how our body evolved back in the day, so you could have the best possible chance of survival in the event of danger (a predator—in our case, the exams). So avoid downing that bottle of Tropicana juice till the exam is over...and that bottle lying in your dad's alcohol cupboard till you're 21 (or 25, depending on which state you're reading this book in).

On the other hand, don't go in for the exam on an empty stomach, else your body will have no energy for the three-hour stretch ahead of you. Remember, your brain needs energy to be able to think clearly.

Keeping all of this in mind, make sure that you eat at least an hour before you leave for your exam, so that your stomach is not stuffed. As mentioned before, you'll be nervous on the day. The nerves and anxiety will only get worse the closer the exam comes. The anxiety and adrenalin in our body will slow and might even completely stop your digestive system.

An ideal meal, therefore, is one that is light, non-spicy and with enough calories to fuel you. Refer to Chapter 22 (specifically the last portion) for more details.

▸ If possible, try to consume green tea before leaving. It's an antioxidant that's believed to enhance memory performance.

▸ Make sure you've packed your stationery. And definitely make sure you're carrying your exam pass. Carry almonds and some coffee powder with you. Consume both before entering the exam hall. The almonds will give you energy and the coffee shot will give you a caffeine kick, which will help you focus better and prevent your attention from drifting. Be careful not to consume too much coffee, as it can have the opposite effect. One spoonful should be more than sufficient.

▸ Avoid chocolate or sugary foods, as these, while

providing the necessary energy, can also give you a sugar crash in the middle of your exam. If you wish to consume chocolate, stick to dark, low-sugar ones.

During the exam

▶ Don't worry about who's taking how many sheets. That's one of the biggest distractions for most students during an exam.

▶ Focus on yourself and tune out the rest of the world.

▶ Stick to the time limits that you've practised adhering to.

▶ If it's a subject with numbers, triple-check every calculation.

▶ Write neatly—make the examiner's life easy. If possible, use two different-coloured pens—black and blue. Use the colours for headings or definitions vis-à-vis explanations. The examiner will appreciate the extra effort you've made. A happy examiner is better than an annoyed one.

▶ Choose the right questions.

▶ Leave enough time for revision. I can't stress this enough. You'll always catch mistakes (just as our editor did, in this very line, while checking the book on the day it was due to go in for typesetting! Now I'm not quite sure if that's irony or just goes to prove my point, which is that you'll always make mistakes—we all do! And since there's a good chance that you will not have the luxury of having an incredible editor proof your writing during your board exams, remember to leave more than enough time at the end of the paper to do so yourself!).

These are the things I kept track of around the time of my exams. I'm sure that there are countless other things that I probably didn't even realize—try to picture the exam week and day in your mind and identify the main things you would like to keep track of. Like I wrote at the beginning of the chapter, control the things you can and forget about the rest.

31

Addictions

Being the best is an addiction. Once you experience the euphoria of winning, however small the competition in question may be, you won't ever want to let that feeling go. You will want to be the best at everything you do. You will constantly want to revisit that high—it's almost like a drug that you can't live without. A drug, yes, but a good one.

All of a sudden, simply being good stops being good enough.

It starts with the little things. For example, it could be triggered by something as simple as coming to class well prepared for the lecture. Here's where evolution comes to your aid—we humans are inherently lazy creatures. We want to get the maximum result with the minimum possible effort. And while there's nothing wrong with that (we even have a scientific word for it—*efficiency*), it usually results in most of us coming unprepared to class.

By simply spending half an hour studying the notes that you've made and coming prepared to class, you'll find yourself plonked squarely in the lonely (previously thought-to-be-unattainable) quartile to the far right on the bell curve—the mythical, inaccessible world of the first-benchers. (Figure drawn below)

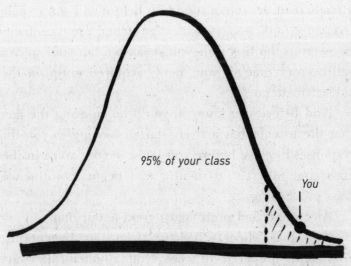

95% of your class

You

Elusive land of the first-benchers

The bell curve is just a fancy word for a drawing that represents where in relation to the rest of the class you currently stand. Assuming that the horizontal X-axis represents your results (or marks), your preparation after following this book will ensure that your results are better than 95 per cent of the rest of the class. Hence your position at the far right of the graph.

And sure, you'll find it a strange, alien land at first. But gradually you'll see a few small changes—you aren't dozing off in the last row any longer, you can anticipate what the teacher is about to discuss because you've already read the topics the night before and you're able to engage in discussions with the teacher. You'll probably be nervous the first time you speak up, but your nerves will be overcome by your newly acquired grasp on the subject matter.

And before you know it, you'll be enjoying the fact that the teacher has actively started looking to you for responses in class. Before you know it, your voice in the classroom will start to matter and begin to influence class proceedings.

And you'll feel pretty darn good about that.

And that wheel will have begun its revolutions: You come prepared to class, you automatically start to get involved. You start to get involved in class, you learn more. You learn more from class, you do better in your tests. You do better in your tests, you start gaining confidence in your approach. You start gaining confidence in your approach, you don't mind working harder, because you can see the results for yourself. You start working harder, your results improve further... And so the wheel continues to roll...

So you see, it's all about the little things.

32

Connecting the Dots: Why We're Doing What We're Doing

Now that we've come so far, I believe it's important for us to revisit exactly what we've gone through and why each step will help us reach our goal. What we've tried to do over the last 200 odd pages is ramp up our preparation, so that come the final day, we're as ready as we'll ever be.

What We're Doing	Why We're Doing It
We start off by laying out the plan for the year.	1. To track our progress and ensure that we achieve the objectives laid out for each stage. 2. To tailor the year to our needs.

We then collect all possible sources of information.	1. To ensure that there's no chance we've left anything out or will be caught by surprise on the day of the exams.
We analyse the books we have to highlight the relevant parts.	1. To make sure that we don't focus our energies on the parts that aren't required. 2. To choose the best parts from each book. 3. To get our first introduction to the syllabus and read everything from start to finish.
We then take time to make notes.	1. To condense all the sources into one concise, easy-to-read notebook. 2. To get into the habit of writing, as it is a written exam, after all. 3. As a byproduct, we revise the entire syllabus.
We revise the notes in class.	1. To optimally utilize 1,170 hours that we might have otherwise wasted. (It also works as a detailed chapter-wise revision)

We make flash cards and start using them every night before bed.	1. To break any rhythm or pattern that we might have fallen into. 2. To list out any problem concepts/definitions/dates, etc. that we can practise quickly and easily at the end of the day. 3. Because they're fun.
We take the best possible tuition within our constraints (if required).	1. To erase any doubts. 2. To get personalized attention. 3. To discuss and debate ideas with a student group of three to six to improve our concepts.
We start solving questions (the Last Ten Years' Papers, question banks, school exam papers, and then the Last Ten Years' Papers again)	1. To get used to writing answers. 2. To break the monotony of revision.
We start using a timer and solve a few full question papers and simulate the final day to the best of our abilities.	1. To get as close to the real experience as possible. 2. To make sure our answers are of the perfect length and make adjustments, if required.

	3. As a byproduct, we will be familiar with the proceedings on the last day, which will reduce our nervousness.
Give the exam.	To top the boards, of course!

As you might have noticed, nothing in this book will have come as a revelation. There's nothing written in here that's some incredible life-altering hack. But the thing is: nothing in life really is. You can't build a great body with a magical protein supplement. Even those who take performance-enhancing drugs only attain the level that they are at through years of hard work and sweat. Nobody becomes a famous musician overnight, without years and years of struggling in anonymity. It's true what they say: It takes years to become an 'overnight success'.

Most of the things written in this book aren't anything special or things that will yield magical results, when viewed in isolation. A lot of them will be fairly obvious and will make you roll your eyes as you read them, thinking, '*I don't need to read this in a book—I already know this.*' But sometimes, we need the obvious spelt out for us, or it is often easy to miss. And it's invariably only obvious in retrospect.

And while a lot of people will definitely be doing some of the things mentioned in this book, probably in isolation, very few will be able to connect the dots and do them all together. It's when you manage to add up all these simple, obvious things that you end up with something special. That's what this book will help you accomplish.

To quote my dad, 'Trifles make perfection, son, but perfection is no trifle.'

At the end of the day, there is no magic formula, or, to steal a line from *Kung Fu Panda*, 'There is no secret ingredient.' The magic lies in you and the effort that you will put in. And while you'll have to work hard, you'll also have to work smart, because often, sad as it may be, working hard simply isn't good enough. You'll have to connect the dots, as I managed to do. Hopefully, my experiences will show you that it isn't anything radical or fancy, but just a matter of small steps that'll get you to your goal.

Remember, it's a marathon, not a sprint.

TIMELINE CHART

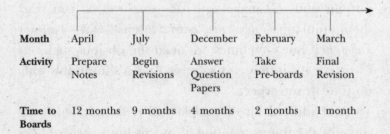

Month	April	July	December	February	March
Activity	Prepare Notes	Begin Revisions	Answer Question Papers	Take Pre-boards	Final Revision
Time to Boards	12 months	9 months	4 months	2 months	1 month

33

Looking Back: Was It All Worth It?

Looking back, was it worth all the hours and the effort? Maybe you find yourself wondering what the payout will be at the end of the day.

Was it worth it?

Allow me to answer that question for you. Without doubt it was.

I do feel inclined to add that because of the way I had structured my preparation year, it didn't feel like a punishment in the slightest. I actually ended up enjoying every second of my board year. And every time I wondered whether it made sense to put in the effort or found my morale flagging, I saw the improvements in my abilities. I saw myself getting better—and that made me feel good. It made me proud and push on. I was determined to give it everything I had—and I did.

And, boy, was it worth it!

That one year helped me get into the college of my dreams. In fact, it laid out an array of choices in front of me when it came to colleges—I had the luxury of saying no to colleges, when it easily could have been the other way round. And as any half-decent economist will tell you—more choice is always better than less choice. Without that one year, I would probably never have gotten a full scholarship to the University of Oxford. Without that one year, I would probably never have gotten scholarship offers from universities in the United States, Yale being one of them. Without that one year, I would never have received a national-level award from the chief minister of Uttarakhand. I would never have received numerous city- and state-level awards from school councils and associations. I would never have found myself giving interviews on television and would never have seen my (pimpled) face in newspapers, magazine covers and photo-ops. Without that one year, I would probably never have gotten one of the highest-paying and most prestigious jobs in India at my level at McKinsey & Company. And I would have most definitely never gotten the chance to have lunch with CEOs of multinational companies at twenty-one.

But most importantly, without that one year, I would

never have been the person I am today.

Because it isn't always just about the tangibles—the scholarships, the jobs or the colleges. It's about so much more than that. Because of the path that my board results set me on, I've met some of the most incredible people, some of whom have become my closest friends, and from friends have gone on to become family. Like I have mentioned before, I met people who inspired me in different ways, people who made me want to become a better human being. I've learnt from them (and still continue to), I've grown with them and flown across the world for their weddings. I've fallen in love and had my heart broken—it's been quite a ride!

The board results were a form of validation, if you can call it that. I became more confident in myself, and that influenced the way others perceived me. I was happy, and that served as a ripple effect that influenced every aspect of my life in a positive way. And most of this would not have been possible without my board results.

So, yes, it was worth it. You can trust me on that.

I will always be grateful for the opportunities that I've received because of my results. It's allowed me the freedom to pursue my passions. I can write because my results gave me the opportunity to do so. I can compose music because I have the opportunity to do so. I can go back to the life of a management consultant because I have the opportunity to do so. You will always have the liberty to choose where you want to take your life, but sometimes, whether you like it or not, the doors just won't open for you. My board result was like a master key that opened a lot of these doors, as it will in your case too.

I will not deny the element of luck. Did I get lucky? I'm sure I did. But as they say, you make your own luck. You have to put yourself in a position that allows you to get lucky. At the end of the day, all you can ask of yourself is that you give it your best shot. Give it everything you've got, because there's nothing more that you can do. Give it your best shot and good things will start to happen. You can count on that.

All the very best, and see you on the other side!

Acknowledgements

I'd like to thank the people without whom this book would have remained an excessively long Word file, tucked away deep in the confines of my hard drive.

There's Randhir Arora, quite possibly one of the most brilliant minds in Dehradun, who took the time to read a kid's manuscript and gave him the encouragement that his 'book' did, in fact, have potential. He doesn't yet know it, but Uncle Randhir is also the reason I cried for the first time in ages when he e-mailed me with the news that Rupa Publications wanted to publish my book. (Okay, that's a lie. I cry through most romcoms.) His e-mail may also be the reason I almost got thrown out of my Oxford College residence on account of my neighbours' complaints of excessive shrieks, yells and sobs (of excitement, I should clarify) coming from the general direction of my room (which is saying something about my reaction, because I've been guilty of aurally traumatizing my neighbours with my guitar-playing for a while now).

Then there's the fantastic team at Rupa Publications India, which, with the help of Mr A.K. Singh, took this from an error-plagued Word file to the book you're currently holding. In particular, I'd like to thank, quite possibly, the best editor in the world, Ujjaini Dasgupta, for being an absolute pleasure to work with. I mean it when I say this book wouldn't be what it is without your contribution, advice and pearls of wisdom.

On to the illustrations, then. I should primarily thank the Internet for inspiration. The Internet and my closest friends, all of whom chipped in to help me make the images you'll see in the book (a little bit of arm-twisting/coercion/bribery may have helped). None of us are professional artists. And, for some strange reason, most of my friends seem to have terrible handwriting— in some cases, so terrible that I was scared to even ask (Poorvi, take note). But it's pointless doing something without the important people in your life being part of it. Which is why Nanya, Pulin, Jacob, Ashoka, Ananya, Anna, Leon, Marcin, Maryna and Unnati—thank you!

To the two people who prevented me from having a meltdown and panicking my way to a cardiac the weekend before the book was to go to print (I write this with less than an hour to go)—Yasho, for patiently sifting through the thousand equally terrible illustrations I concocted (I refrain from using the word *designed*), choosing the best ones and suggesting a few brilliant ideas; and Gugu (or Nandita), for coming up with the most breathtaking work, when all you had were a few hours till the deadline and a bunch of vague WhatsApp messages from the other end of the planet from an author running around his room like a headless chicken—you're incredible.

To Rohit and Harleen, for tolerating me all these years and not resorting to the overwhelming but absolutely understandable urge to stab me with a fork for yet another unwashed dish left on the kitchen slab. (It's possible that I'm writing this under duress, as Rohit hovers ominously around with a recently sharpened kitchen knife, making sure that I say something nice about him.)

Finally, to my wonderful teachers at The Doon School, Dr Kanti Bajpai, our headmaster, for not pulling out his remaining hair, the incredible Doscos that I'm lucky to call my classmates, my family—extended and otherwise—the Soods, Phillips, Upadhayas, Malhotras, Badhwars... And chachu, nanu, amma, bawa, tata and Susan aunty, because we miss you.

And, of course, to the best friends I ever made the day I walked through the gates of St Stephen's College. I don't know where I'd be without you. You know who you are.